PRAISE FOR

Jews Don't Need Jesus
. . . and Other Misconceptions

If the gospel is not for the Jewish people, it's not for anyone, and if Jesus is not the Messiah of Israel, then He's not the Savior of the world. And if Jewish people (or any people) can be saved apart from knowing Jesus as Lord, then His death on the cross was in vain. Sadly, in an effort to repent of spiritual pride and to renounce "Christian" anti-Semitism, many churches today no longer share the gospel with Jewish people, believing that they have their own covenant with God. This book, written by a seasoned Jewish missionary, dispels these misconceptions and calls on Christians everywhere to proclaim the good news about Jesus the Messiah, to the Jew first.

MICHAEL L. BROWN
Author, *Answering Jewish Objections to Jesus*

That Jesus is the Savior of the world who is the Messiah and Son of God is a truth that cannot be rejected. Avi Snyder argues well that bringing the gospel of Jesus Christ to the Jews as well as to the Gentiles is still of paramount importance. The Bible teaches that God chose to work with Israel in the past, that a remnant is still being saved today, and that "all Israel" will be saved in the future. That salvation is found in no one other than in Jesus the Messiah, the Son of God.

MARK L. BAILEY
President, Dallas Theological Seminary

In our clouded, jumbled world, an increasing number of Christians are viewing Jewish evangelism with a skeptical eye. The sad result is not surprising—fewer followers of Jesus are seeking to tell Jews about Him. Armed with forty years of experience and the mandate of Scripture, Avi Snyder confronts and dismantles each objection. This valuable book brings a needed focus back to the church: the gospel is first "to the Jews."

J. PAUL NYQUIST
President, Moody Bible Institute

As the pastor of a Bible-believing church and a Jewish believer in Jesus myself, I wholeheartedly recommend this book! It effectively presents the case to Christians for including Jewish people in their evangelism efforts and can only enhance the local church's missions mandate.

LON SOLOMON
Senior Pastor, McLean Bible Church, McLean, VA

If I found a treasure, hidden in a field, which would help to meet all of my deepest needs, would I keep it to myself? No way! I would want to share it with everyone, including those who first owned it, and everyone else. That is the way it is with the good news of Jesus. I am a debtor with a debt to repay—to God for His great gift, to the people He first chose as His own, and to everyone everywhere who is seeking life in all its fullness.

LEIGHTON FORD
President, Leighton Ford Ministries

Sharing the good news of Messiah Jesus with others is the joy and the duty of every Christ follower. In the Great Commission, Jesus sent His apostles to make disciples of all nations. As they went forth to fulfill this calling, they preached to the Jews first, and then to the Gentiles. On the basis of this biblical precedent and of the integrity of the Bible, it is Avi Snyder's burning conviction that the gospel should be brought to people of every background, including the Jewish people. Sharing the truth of the Messiahship of Jesus and inviting others to follow Him is therefore not an option, but a necessity, born out of truth and love. In this passionate plea, Avi bares his heart and pleads for a new commitment to evangelism. A must read for all who desire to think biblically about evangelism. As a Christian from Germany, I stand convicted by the arguments of this Messianic Jewish brother.

ROLAND S. WERNER
Author, church planter, Bible translator, and Professor for Theology in a Global Context at the Evangelische Hochschule Tabor, Marburg, Germany

The biblical record is clear and passionate on this need—Jewish people need to be saved and brought to the knowledge of the truth. Our church has stepped up our efforts and stand with Jewish Christians in Israel to help spread the Jesus message. We give it as much focus as our commitment to reach Arab Muslims. Why would it be any different? This is vital and urgent. Dear Lord, use this book to light a gospel flame for every Jew in the world.

LON ALLISON
Author, professor, and Pastor of Teaching and Outreach, Wheaton Bible Church

Avi Snyder was a successful Broadway actor until Christ apprehended him for His own. When I first met him, Avi was developing a one-man drama based on the life and message of the apostle Paul. I was amazed at how Avi used mostly the text of Paul's epistles to powerfully portray this greatest of missionaries. Ever since, I have watched the same zeal and love for God displayed in Avi's life as he founded Jewish mission works in five different countries around the world. Everywhere Avi goes he inspires others to live passionately for Christ. This book is his magnum opus. It captures the passion of the apostle Paul and takes us through the Scriptures with the same mastery and zeal Paul did. Thank you, Avi, for living and writing boldly, biblically, and powerfully for the sake of the salvation of Israel.

DAVID BRICKNER
Executive Director, Jews for Jesus

JEWS DON'T NEED JESUS

& OTHER MISCONCEPTIONS

Reflections of a Jewish Believer

AVI SNYDER

MOODY PUBLISHERS

CHICAGO

Edited by Connor Sterchi
Interior and cover design: Erik M. Peterson
Cover Image: Cover painting by Maurice Gottlieb, *Jews Praying in the Synagogue on Yom Kippur* (1878)
Author Photo: Niek Stam

ISBN: 978-0-8024-1656-8

We hope you enjoy this book from Moody Publishers. Our goal is to provide high-quality, thought-provoking books and products that connect truth to your real needs and challenges. For more information on other books and products written and produced from a biblical perspective, go to www.moodypublishers.com or write to:

Moody Publishers
820 N. LaSalle Boulevard
Chicago, IL 60610

1 3 5 7 9 10 8 6 4 2

Printed in the United States of America

To Ruth, and the Martins

CONTENTS

THE REAL REASONS FOR CHOOSING NOT TO SPEAK

Foreword

EVEN BEFORE I READ THIS BOOK, I felt a deep desire to write a foreword for a work on this topic. Now that I have read it, that desire burns all the more.

Before I knew this book was being written, I had said to the content team at our web-based ministry, desiringGod.org, "I want us to do more for the cause of Jewish evangelism." Why was I stirred again with this burden? And all the more now that I have read this book?

Nearly 60,000 Jewish people live in the Twin Cities metropolitan area I call home. More than five million live in the United States, and over 14 million in the world. The vast majority of them do not embrace Jesus as their Messiah and Savior. In fact, they believe that to do so would mean the end to their true Jewishness.

Even though thousands of Jewish people embraced Jesus in the early days of the Christian church (three thousand in Acts 2:41; at least another two thousand in Acts 4:4), some also claimed that Christians aimed to "destroy [the Temple] and . . . change the customs that Moses delivered to us" (Acts 6:14). Nevertheless, the first and greatest Christian missionary, a Jew himself and former Pharisee, the apostle Paul, protested that he was "saying nothing but what the prophets and Moses said would come to pass: that the Christ must suffer and that, by being the first to rise from the dead, he would proclaim light both to our people and to the Gentiles" (Acts 26:22–23).

There have always been Jewish people in every generation who have believed this—that Jesus did not "come to abolish the Law or the Prophets . . . but to fulfill them" (Matt. 5:17). But the great sadness of true Christians—along with humiliation and grief at the way Jews have been treated through the centuries—is that most Jewish people still turn away from Jesus as the one who fulfills the promises of God in the Jewish Scriptures.

This rejection brought anguish to that great Jewish missionary and apostle. The most poignant words Paul ever wrote concerned his Jewish kinsmen: "I am speaking the truth in Christ—I am not lying; my conscience bears me witness in the Holy Spirit—that I have great sorrow and unceasing anguish in my heart. For I could wish that I myself were accursed and cut off from Christ for the sake of my brothers, my kinsmen according to the flesh" (Rom. 9:1–3).

"Great sorrow and unceasing anguish"! This is simply astonishing. "Great" and "unceasing." Nothing else burdened Paul like this. I have often wondered how he kept on going. He had evidently learned a rare secret—that it is possible to be profoundly restful and content at the same time as being profoundly sorrowful (Phil. 4:11–12). In fact, he said he lived "as sorrowful, yet always rejoicing" (2 Cor. 6:10).

Out of this mysterious mingling of joy and sorrow, his prayers overflowed for his Jewish people: "Brothers, my heart's desire and prayer to God for them is that they may be saved" (Rom. 10:1). Which means that his sorrow and his prayers were moved by the heart-wrenching reality that they were not "saved"—that Jews who reject Jesus reject eternal life. When Paul's message about Jesus was rejected by the Jewish leaders in Antioch of Pisidia, he said, "It was necessary that the word of God be spoken first to you. Since you thrust it aside and *judge yourselves unworthy of eternal life*, behold, we are turning to the Gentiles" (Acts 13:46).

This is the heart of the matter, and why I was drawn to Avi Snyder's book even before I read it. The good news of Jesus, coming and dying for sinners and rising again, was for Israel first. But that privilege did not mean Jewish people would escape judgment if they rejected the good news of Jesus.

A priority is given to the Jewish people in the Christian mission. Jesus Himself came first to "the lost sheep of the house of Israel" (Matt. 10:6; 15:24), not to the Gentiles. Only later did the good news for Israel spill over for all the nations (Matt. 8:11; 21:43; 28:19–20). The first missionaries of the Christian church preserved that priority for Jewish people in evangelism. "The gospel . . . is the power of God for salvation to everyone who believes, *to the Jew first and also to the Greek*" (Rom. 1:16). This was God's design: "God, having raised up his servant [Jesus], sent him to you [Israel] *first,* to bless you by turning every one of you from your wickedness" (Acts 3:26).

But neither Jesus nor His apostles taught that this priority meant Israel would be rescued from judgment in spite of turning away from Jesus. Jesus did not come as one among many ways to God. He came as the true and only Jewish Messiah and Mediator between God and man. "I am the way, and the truth, and the life. No one comes to the Father except through me" (John 14:6). And He taught plainly that to reject Him was to reject God. Accepting Him was the litmus test of whether anyone's claim to know God was real. For example, He said,

- "You know neither me nor my Father. If you knew me, you would know my Father also." (John 8:19)
- "Whoever does not honor the Son does not honor the Father who sent him." (John 5:23)
- "I know that you do not have the love of God within you. I have come in my Father's name, and you do not receive me." (John 5:42–43)
- "If God were your Father, you would love me, for I came from God and I am here." (John 8:42)
- No one who denies the Son has the Father. Whoever confesses the Son has the Father also. (1 John 2:23)
- "It is written in the Prophets, 'And they will all be taught by God.' Everyone who has heard and learned from the Father comes to me." (John 6:45)

So it is not only the apostle Paul who says that the Jewish people who reject Jesus as the Messiah also reject eternal life, but Jesus Himself said the same thing: "Whoever believes in the Son has eternal life; whoever does not obey the Son shall not see life, but the wrath of God remains on him" (John 3:36).

But in spite of these weighty warnings, the New Testament holds out spectacular hope for the people of Israel. The apostle Peter calls Israel to "repent . . . that your sins may be blotted out, that times of refreshing may come from the presence of the Lord, and that he may send the Christ appointed for you, Jesus" (Acts 3:19–20).

Then, more fully than anyone in the New Testament, Paul unfolds the hope of the gospel for Israel. Not only is there a "remnant, chosen by grace" in every generation who will believe on Jesus (Rom. 11:5), but also the day is coming when the "fullness" of Israel will turn to Jesus and be saved (Rom. 11:12 NKJV).

As a Gentile, I am, so to speak, a wild olive branch, not a natural one. The "olive tree" of the Abrahamic covenant is not "naturally" mine. But because Jesus is the Messiah for all peoples, I am grafted in "contrary to nature." I owe my salvation to inclusion in the Jewish tree! With this analogy, Paul argues, "If you [Gentiles] were cut from what is by nature a wild olive tree, and grafted, contrary to nature, into a cultivated olive tree, *how much more* will these, the natural [Jewish] branches, be grafted back into their own olive tree" (Rom. 11:24). Then, stunningly, he says, "In this way *all Israel* will be saved" (Rom. 11:26).

This New Testament picture of the *glorious future* of Israel *in* relationship to Jesus, together with the picture of the *tragic present* of Israel *out* of relationship to Jesus, is what made me want to write the foreword for this book even before I read it.

Then I read it. Only a Jewish person with a deep love for his people could have written this book. I say that not only because of the personal empathy that abounds in the book, but also because only a Jewish person could see so clearly the objections raised against sharing the message of Jesus Christ. Which means that the book is emotionally and intellectually tuned into the post-Holocaust, pluralistic world, especially in the West.

Avi Snyder has experienced at least sixteen objections to Jewish and Gentile efforts to win Jewish people to faith in Jesus as the Messiah and Savior. I say "experienced," rather than merely "heard," because he speaks from inside real relationships, where these objections are deeply felt. He writes insightful, biblical, personal answers to each objection.

Nothing is merely theoretical. For example, if you say, "It is impossible for a Jewish person to believe on Jesus after the horrors of the Holocaust," he will say,

> I wish I could invite you to ask Manfred and Laura Wertheim, Rachmiel Frydland, Vera Schlamm, Eleazer Erbach, Rose Price, or Carl Flesch whether or not the Holocaust made it impossible for Jewish people to come to faith. These are just some of the many Jewish people who went through the inferno of the Holocaust but came to faith in Yeshua.

If you say, "You just don't realize the unspeakable history of the way the Christian church has treated Jewish people throughout the last two thousand years," he pours out his lament:

> So many crimes against the Jewish people can be traced to the anti-Jewish teachings of the church: charges of deicide by church fathers; legal writs against us during the Dark Ages; the slaughter of European Jewish communities by Crusaders on their way to "liberate" the Holy Land; the expulsions, tortures, executions, and

forced baptisms of the Inquisition; the blood libels and pogroms in Europe and Russia. Moreover, anti-Semitic teaching in the church was a significant factor in the support and condoning of the Nazis shown by many in the church during the Holocaust. It's little wonder why we Jews find it so hard to give Yeshua a fair and impartial hearing.

If you say, "Faith in Jesus as the Messiah will be the end of my Jewish existence," he says,

> Faith in Yeshua is not a threat to Jewish existence but an affirmation of our identity as Jews. The God who saved us through our faith in Jesus is the God who deepens our Jewish identity through that same faith. More often than not, Jewish people who believe in Yeshua experience a heightened commitment to their Jewish heritage and roots. By coming to Jesus, we discover that we've come home.

And if you say, as one man did, "I feel we Germans have forfeited the right to talk with Jews about the Lord," he gently disagrees:

> "You not only have the right," I offered. "You have the responsibility." I went on to tell him how I believed that God was bringing the Jewish people back to Germany for at least three reasons: because of His love for the Jewish people, because of His love for the German church, and because of His love for the German people. "God wants my people to hear the

gospel and be saved. He wants German believers to know the joy of being used by God to bring His people to Himself. He wants *Germans* to hear the gospel from Jewish lips. And I think He wants the world to see Jews and Germans proclaiming the gospel together. What a testimony of the love of the Lord. What a testimony of the reconciling power of the cross.

A book like this has always been needed, not only because of the misunderstandings and legitimate fears of Jewish people, but also because of the failures and fears of Christians. But today—a day when whole Christian denominations are renouncing (and denouncing) all efforts to win Jewish people to faith in Jesus—this book is more needed than ever.

The note it strikes is crystal clear. It is not love to "follow your heart" if your heart builds a theology that contradicts the truth.

> Eighty years ago, that tendency of following the heart, then constructing the theology led to the abandonment, betrayal, and destruction of one-third of my people. Today, that same tendency is placing the Jewish people's spiritual well-being in the gravest peril. Ironically, the first instance occurred as a result of undisguised hate but today it's occurring in the name of love.

Those are strong words. But Jewish people who know their Scriptures are used to strong words. "My people are destroyed for lack of knowledge" (Hos. 4:6). It is not hate or ignorance or naiveté or presumption that motivates Avi Snyder to plead with his people to turn to Jesus and to plead with us to join him. It is love.

> For Zion's sake I will not keep silent, and for Jerusalem's sake I will not keep quiet, until her righteousness goes forth like brightness, and her salvation like a torch that is burning. (Isa. 62:1–2)

As a Gentile, I have felt moved by this book to love Jesus and to love Jewish people better. Surely Avi Snyder is right:

> Silence about the gospel is not love. Silence is the enemy of the salvation of my people. Silence is the enemy of the salvation of any people.

JOHN PIPER
Founder and teacher
desiringGod.org

Introduction

One Is Right, One Is Wrong

IN THE AUTUMN OF 1991, my wife Ruth and I moved to the Soviet Union, just as it was falling apart. Some of our friends were afraid that they'd never see us again, and I'll admit that Ruth and I were very uncertain about the situation into which we were going to leap. Only a couple of weeks earlier, Soviet hardliners had seized the "apostate" General Secretary of the Communist Party, Mikhail Gorbachev, in a bid to reinstate the toppling USSR. In the wake of his arrest and subsequent release, chaos seemed to reign.

But Ruth and I believed that this would be the perfect time to come to the region with the good news. People needed to know that a hope and a future awaited anyone who repented and openly confessed that the Messiah Yeshua had died for our sins and had risen from the dead. So, along with our three children and one colleague, we moved to Odessa, Ukraine, with two goals in mind: to bring the gospel to our Jewish people, and to establish a Jewish evangelistic ministry comprised of Soviet-born staff.

Mr. Reiner (not his real name) had come to Odessa for a different reason. He believed that God had called him in a vision to help Jewish people make Aliyah (immigrate to Israel) from the USSR. When he learned about my presence in Odessa, he invited me to his hotel room to talk.

But as soon as we met, we discovered a misunderstanding that needed to be cleared up right away. Mr. Reiner had assumed that I was a local messianic leader, and he'd sought me out so that he could urge me to flee. He clearly loved the Jewish people, and like the angels who visited Lot just prior to the coming of God's judgment on Sodom and Gomorrah, he wanted to help my family and me escape.

After listening to his pleas and plans, I let him know that I was a Jewish missionary originally from the States, and that I'd only recently relocated to Ukraine to tell our people about the Lord. Then I proposed a way for us to work together. I explained that God had already allowed us to see a good deal of encouraging fruit in our first two and a half months of outreach. Jewish people were giving their hearts to Jesus, and a core of staff and volunteers had come together, intent on proclaiming the gospel so long as the window of opportunity remained open. If Mr. Reiner planned to bring even more Jewish people to the port of Odessa from other parts of the USSR, then why not combine our efforts? My team and I would be delighted, I said, to share the good news with these Jewish émigrés before they left for Israel. That way, they could travel with the gospel sown in their hearts. The more I talked and listened to my own words, the more excited I became. It sounded like a good idea to me.

But apparently, it sounded like something else to Mr. Reiner. He rose stiffly and spoke in a heavy voice, like a teacher reprimanding a disobedient student. "I have given my word that I will have nothing to do with missionary activity," he said. Then he took out a folder, laid it on the bed, and showed me with solemn pride the documents he'd signed, pledging to keep silent about Jesus.

I stared at the documents, unable to speak. But after a moment, I found my voice again. "A Jewish person who dies in the USSR without knowing Yeshua enters eternity separated from God," I began. Then I added, "If you help him move from the USSR to Israel, and if he dies in Israel without knowing Yeshua, he still enters eternity separated from God."

Mr. Reiner winced. "Actually," he said, "we don't know what happens to a Jewish person who dies without knowing the Lord."

"But we do," I pressed, softly but ardently. I reminded him of the words of Hebrews 9:27—words written to us Jews: "it is appointed for men to die once and after this comes judgment."

"Theologically, you might be right," Mr. Reiner said. "But I feel a check in my spirit." He used a Christian idiom that was popular at the time. It meant, "Despite what you say, the Spirit tells me that you're wrong."

"The check that you feel isn't coming from the Lord," I told him. How did I know? Because the Spirit of God doesn't speak a message to our hearts that contradicts what He's already spoken through His Word. That's why we're exhorted to test the spirits (1 John 4:1), and the litmus test is the written Word of God.

We were trying to speak gingerly with each other, because

The wall between us was whether or not the Jewish people needed to hear the gospel as urgently as everyone else. To him, the matter was open to debate, and therefore not so crucial. To me, the matter was settled and of paramount importance.

neither of us wanted our passions to provoke a heated debate. But there really wasn't anywhere else for the conversation to go. Awkwardly, we shook hands and wished God's blessing on each other's lives.

Then I walked out of his room.

The issue standing between us wasn't whether or not Jewish people should make Aliyah. Both of us believed in that. Nor was the issue the depth of our mutual love for the Jewish people. Rather, the dividing point was his pledge to keep silent about the message of salvation. The wall between us was whether or not the Jewish people needed to hear the gospel as urgently as everyone else. To him, the matter was open to debate, and therefore not so crucial. To me, the matter was settled and of paramount importance. As far as I was concerned, bringing the gospel to my people amounted to a matter of life and death.

One of us was right, and one of us was wrong.

If Yeshua is not the Jewish Messiah and the only Savior of the nations, and if He is not the promised Redeemer whom the Father has sent "to restore the preserved ones of Israel" and to be "a light of the nations" (Isa. 49:6), then bringing His message to the Jewish people is possibly the gravest threat to our physical and spiritual well-being. Why? Because if Jesus is not who He claimed to be, then urging Jews to believe in Him is an invitation to apostasy and an attack on our very existence. If Jesus is an imposter, then belief in Him threatens our survival as a distinct people, chosen by God.

But what if He *is* the prophet like Moses whom God promised to raise up? What if He *is* the One whom God commanded the Jewish people to heed? And what if we Jews *will* be held accountable by God if we fail to listen to what He's said, just as Deuteronomy 18:18–19 warns? Then to withhold the message of the gospel from the Jewish people specifically because we're Jews is not an act of love. It's probably the most anti-Jewish act that a Christian can commit.

This is not an easy matter to consider, but we can't push it aside. Either He's a blessing for Jews, or He's a blight. There's really no middle ground, just as there was no middle ground between Mount Gerizim and Mount Ebal.

Also, if Jesus is not the Messiah of Israel, then He's not the Christ of the nations. That means that Christians who worship Him are guilty of idolatry, and they'll be judged by the God of Abraham, Isaac, and Jacob for worshiping a man who claimed to be God (John 10:33).

It's likely to get harder and harder for Christians who love the Jewish people to stand firm in their conviction that Jews need Jesus as much as everyone else.

Ultimately, it comes down to this: either Jesus is Lord of all, or Jesus is not Lord at all. Either He must be worshiped, adored, and obeyed by Jews and non-Jews alike, or He must be rejected by all as a false savior. Either everyone must hear the message, or no one needs to know His name.

If you're not yet a believer in Jesus, you'll quickly discover that this book deals candidly with a passionate dispute between people who already acknowledge Yeshua as the promised Messiah. But there's a foundational question that needs to be asked and answered first: Is Jesus the Messiah or not? Or, as a Jewish man called John the Immerser (the Baptizer) asked nearly two thousand years ago, "Are You the Expected One, or shall we look for someone else?" (Matt. 11:3). I hope you'll read this book with that fundamental question in mind.

If you do believe in Jesus, and if you agree that only the gospel rescues people from sin and death, then I hope the words that follow will encourage you to remain strong in your commitment to that biblical truth, no matter what price you might have to pay. It's likely to get harder and harder for Christians who love the Jewish people to stand firm in their conviction that Jews need Jesus as much as everyone else. As more of the world turns against us Jews, just as the Bible predicts, some Christians will be tempted to disavow the cause of Jewish evangelism as a way of expressing their solidarity with the Jewish people. They'll want to affirm whatever the Jewish people affirm, and they'll want to distance themselves from whatever the Jewish people push away.

True love always seeks the beloved's best, even when the beloved fails to understand.

Unfortunately, as far as most Jews are concerned, Jewish evangelism belongs in the "push away" category. I hope this book will deepen your resolve to stand up for the cause of "Jesus for the Jews," despite any unpopularity you may face from the very Jewish people you love. True love always seeks the beloved's best, even when the beloved fails to understand.

If you're a sincere Christian, but you don't endorse the cause of Jewish evangelism, then I hope you'll consider with an open mind whether my arguments are true to what the Scriptures teach. Actually, I'm hoping for more. Yeshua said, "no one comes to the Father but through Me" (John 14:6). I earnestly hope you'll see that those words are true and necessary for all people, including for His fellow Jews. And I earnestly hope you'll find the courage to advocate for the cause of bringing the gospel to the Jewish people, despite the reproach that you'll undoubtedly share with Jesus and with us Jews who already believe.

Perhaps like Mr. Reiner, you view silence as a gesture of love. However, as Messianic Jews, we cannot be silent, because our love compels us to speak. Two loves—one arguing for silence, the other pleading for utterance.

One is right, and one is wrong.

WHAT THE
BIBLE HAS TO SAY

CHAPTER 1

Good News and Bad News

IF WE'RE GOING TO consider whether the gospel message is relevant to the Jewish people, then we ought to start with an understanding of the message itself. The word *gospel* means "good news," but in reality, the message is both good and bad.

The good news is that God loves each one of us so passionately that He's provided a way for us to be forgiven and restored to a personal, eternal relationship with Him. The bad news is that each one of us is cut off from God because of our sin (Isa. 59:1–2). We're born with rebellious hearts, and we practice that rebellion throughout our entire lives.

There's a Jewish teaching that says we actually possess two natures: *ha yetzer hara* and *ha yetzer tov*—the evil inclination, and the good. It's an appealing idea to think that we're born with the scales set at "even," and that we can control the course of our lives for the good, if we follow a certain path. The path for us Jews, according to this teaching, is the path of pursuing a life of strict obedience to the Law of Moses.

But let's be honest with ourselves. As children, did any of us need to be taught how to be jealous or selfish? Did we have to be taught how to desire what wasn't our own, to blame others, to conceal what we'd done when we knew it wasn't right, or to deny it or lie about it when we were found out? All of that came very naturally to every one of us.

We don't have two inclinations; we have one. Tragically, we're infected with a sinful and rebellious nature from birth. It's our spiritual DNA, and it's killing us.

By contrast, we needed to be taught to trust and share, to be kind and forgiving. We needed to learn to choose the good over the evil because, sadly, evil is our default. It's our natural bent.

We don't have two inclinations; we have one. Tragically, we're infected with a sinful and rebellious nature from birth. It's our spiritual DNA, and it's killing us.

It's because of our rebellion that our lives feel bankrupt and pointless, no matter what we do. By turning away from God, we've divorced ourselves from the only One who can give our lives real meaning and genuine affirmation for a job well done. Solomon knew the misery of living a pointless life that comes from being cut off from God, and he cried, "Vanity of vanities! All is vanity!" (Eccl. 1:2).

It's because of our rebellion that our relationships fail to satisfy us, and why they fall apart. Since our primary relationship with God has been severed by our sin, every other relationship with anyone else falls victim to sin as well. In short, we're unfaithful to each other because we're unfaithful to God. And even if we try to change, sin holds so tightly on to every aspect of our lives that we're powerless to break the grip. Caught in that grip, we grovel through pointless lives and broken relationships, with no power to change. And we are heading toward a godless eternity. That's the bad news.

RESCUED

But here's the good news: God loves each one of us so deeply and so intensely, that He provided a way for us to be forgiven for our rebellion, rescued from our plight, and restored to a proper relationship with Him. The Father sent the Son, Yeshua (Jesus' Hebrew name) the Messiah, in order to die as the payment for our sins and rise from the dead, just as Moses and the prophets foretold. When He died, He took upon Himself the punishment of God that our rebellion deserves. No wonder He cried out from the cross in unspeakable agony, "My God, my God, why have You forsaken me?" (Ps. 22:1). Yes, He was pointing us to the prophecy about His crucifixion so that we might know that everything was going just as the Father had planned. But those words were also a cry of unimaginable emotional pain. In that moment, the Son was experiencing the horror of being utterly forsaken and abandoned by the Father. That abandonment is hell.

Yeshua's anguish should have been ours. But He took that agony upon Himself so that we might never know that torment and never utter that cry. He willingly endured the punishment that we deserve when He gave His life as the payment for our sins.

> He was pierced through for our transgressions, He was crushed for our iniquities . . . He was cut off out of the land of the living for the transgression of my people, to whom the stroke was due. (Isa. 53:5, 8)

JESUS DIED FOR OUR SINS

But He didn't stay dead. He came back from the grave, as prophesied by King David in Psalm 16:10, and as promised by Yeshua Himself in Matthew 12:39–40. His resurrection proves that His claims about being our Messiah are true, because His resurrection is the very sign of confirmation that He told us He would give. His resurrection also lets us know with certainty that the debt we owe to God has been paid on our behalf, if we repent and believe. It's a legal concept, and it's easy to grasp: just as criminals are released from prison after they've "paid their debt" to society, so Yeshua was released from the prison of death as proof that our debt has been paid, if we receive that payment as our own.

Jesus exchanges our separation *from* God with a new relationship *with* God—an intimate, everlasting relationship that begins the moment that we repent and believe.

His resurrection assures us of something else. Because He's alive, we can come to Him, and we can be certain that we'll be forgiven, if we approach Him with repentant hearts. This is the greatest comfort that we can ever know.

Consider the agonizing alternative. If Jesus had died but had never risen from the dead, if the one I've offended is no longer alive, then I can never hear Him say, "I forgive you." I can never be free from my guilt, even if I regret my crimes with every fiber of my being. A corpse can't forgive.

But Yeshua isn't dead. He's alive. And when we ask Him to forgive us, He speaks the most wonderful words that our hearts will ever hear. "Your sins are forgiven."

If we believe that Yeshua died for our sins and rose from the dead, if we repent of our sins and ask Him to forgive us, and if we openly profess Him as Lord, then He rescues us from the power that sin exercises over our present lives, and from the eternal punishment that we deserve—being utterly and eternally forsaken by the Father. He replaces our chronically rebellious hearts with new hearts that want to obey. His Spirit, living within us, actually empowers us to obey. He fills the void of our empty lives with a purpose and a plan. He makes our relationships right by teaching us to love Him with all our heart, soul, and strength, and to love each other as we love ourselves. He exchanges our separation *from* God with a new relationship *with* God—an intimate, everlasting relationship that begins the moment that we repent and believe.

The Bible calls this relationship the gift of eternal life. But we don't have to wait for eternity in order to experience it. It's ours even now, when we hear the message of the gospel and repent.

That's the good news. That's the gospel. That's the truth. And it is a message that all people, including the Jewish people, need to hear and receive.

CHAPTER 2

If Jews Don't Need Jesus, Then Why . . . ?

I've been told . . .

> "Jews don't need to believe in Jesus in order to be saved."

IF IT'S TRUE THAT Jews don't need Jesus for salvation, then why did Jesus and His disciples proclaim the gospel so passionately and so persistently to their fellow Jews?

We read in the gospel of Matthew that Jesus traveled throughout Galilee, "teaching in their synagogues and proclaiming the gospel of the kingdom" (Matt. 4:23). Does the fact that Jesus declared "the gospel of the kingdom" automatically drive us to the conclusion that we must bring the gospel to the Jewish people today? Not necessarily. It could be argued that He proclaimed the gospel as an *option*, not as a necessity. Or, it could be argued that His message and activity simply placed Him in the company of the Old Testament–style prophets. "Yes, Jesus called for His people to repent, but so did a host of other messengers before Him."

But when we consider other statements that He uttered, then a clearer picture emerges about the specific content of His message and the unique claims that He made about Himself. In John 8:24, we're told that Jesus explained, "Unless you believe that I am He, you will die in your sins." And in John 14:6, one of the best known passages from the New Testament, Jesus declared, "I am the way, and the truth, and the life; no one comes to the Father but through Me."

Jesus delivered the gospel message to the Jewish people not as an option but as a necessity.

In both of these statements, He made unique claims about Himself, and He was speaking to His fellow Jews. It's hard to avoid the obvious conclusion: Jesus delivered the gospel message to the Jewish people not as an option but as a necessity.

". . . AS THE FATHER HAS SENT ME, I ALSO SEND YOU . . ." (JOHN 20:21)

Jesus not only practiced Jewish evangelism Himself; He commanded His followers to do the same. In Matthew 10:6–7, we're told that when He first began to send the apostles out to proclaim the gospel message, He instructed them to go exclusively to the "lost sheep of the house of Israel. And as you go, preach, saying, 'The kingdom of heaven is at hand.'"

The book of Acts makes it clear that the apostles and early disciples heeded His commandment and engaged in Jewish evangelism wherever they carried the good news. For example, on the very first Shavuot (Pentecost) after the resurrection of the Lord, Peter seized the opportunity to tell a predominantly Jewish crowd from virtually every region of the known world, "let all the house of Israel know for certain that God has made Him [Jesus] both Lord and Christ" (Acts 2:36).

As a result of his unceasing evangelistic activity among his fellow Jews, Peter ultimately found himself standing as a prisoner before the Sanhedrin, the seventy-one religious leaders of the Jewish people. And on that occasion, he declared, "there is no other name [besides Yeshua] under heaven that has been given among men by which we must be saved" (Acts 4:12). Once again, we need to take note of the content of the message, and the context in which it was delivered. Peter emphatically declared that Jesus is the only way of salvation, and he made that declaration to his fellow Jews (specifically, to the Jewish high court).

PETER, APOSTLE
"TO THE CIRCUMCISED" (GAL. 2:7)

In Galatians 2:7–8, Paul speaks of Peter's apostleship to the "circumcised," or to the Jewish people. By definition, an apostle is a person who has been sent out with a message. The message that the apostles carried was the good news that Yeshua had died for our sins and had risen from the dead. But if Jewish evangelism is unnecessary, then why was Peter ever commissioned by the Lord to be the apostle to the Jews? Why, for that matter, did Peter repeatedly risk his life by declaring a message that his hearers really didn't need to hear?

During the early days of the church, *Gentile* evangelism was the controversial issue (see Acts 11:1–3). *Jewish* evangelism was taken for granted. It was the norm, and no one contested either the activity or the need.

The story doesn't end with Peter, of course. We know that the other apostles and disciples not only proclaimed the gospel to their fellow Jews (Acts 6:7–10; 11:19); we know that many of them thought that the message should be proclaimed *only* to the Jews. Ultimately, it took some heated debate and the intervention of the Holy Spirit Himself to convince those first Jewish believers that they should proclaim the gospel to the Gentiles as well (Acts 11:1–3; 15:6–9, 13–20). In other words, during the early days of the church, *Gentile* evangelism was the controversial issue (see Acts 11:1–3). *Jewish* evangelism was taken for granted. It was the norm, and no one contested either the activity or the need.

". . . TO THE JEW FIRST" (ROM. 1:16)

Paul was called to be the apostle to the Gentiles (Acts 22:21; Gal. 2:7). But even so, the record in Acts reveals that he always began his ministry in every new city by first evangelizing his fellow Jews. In fact, while living among the disciples in Damascus, immediately after coming to faith and long before launching out on his very first missionary journey, Paul "began to proclaim Jesus in the synagogues, saying, 'He is the Son of God'" (Acts 9:20). Then, after returning to Jerusalem, Paul spent his time "talking and arguing with the Hellenistic Jews" (Acts 9:29). What he practiced in Damascus and Jerusalem became his enduring pattern in every city that he visited throughout his entire missionary career. Even in the final chapter of Acts, when Paul was brought to Rome as a prisoner, we're told that he "called together those who were the leading men of the Jews . . . and he was explaining to them by solemnly testifying about the kingdom of God and trying to persuade them concerning Jesus, from both the Law of Moses and from the Prophets" (Acts 28:17, 23).

From Damascus to Rome, we always see Paul, the apostle to the Gentiles, proclaiming the gospel "to the Jew first."

"HIM OF WHOM MOSES IN THE LAW AND ALSO THE PROPHETS WROTE" (JOHN 1:45)

Even before Yeshua's first advent, Moses and the prophets pointed us to His coming, delivered His message, and exhorted us to believe. In the Law, God both promised a coming Redeemer and warned the Jewish people about the consequences of failing to receive His words. Speaking to Moses, God explained,

> I will raise up a prophet from among their countrymen like you, and I will put My words in his mouth, and he shall speak to them all that I command him. It shall come about that whoever will not listen to My words which he shall speak in My name, I Myself will require it of him. (Deut. 18:18–19)

If Jews don't need to believe in Jesus, then why did God warn us through Moses of the frightful consequences that would befall us if we failed to believe and heed Yeshua's words?

There's really no ambiguity about what the biblical record reveals. Even so, many misconceptions cloud the issue and undermine the need for Jewish evangelism.

Six centuries after Moses, the prophet Isaiah described the reason for the Suffering Servant's ordeal. Writing as a Jew to other Jews, Isaiah declared, "He was pierced through for our transgressions, He was crushed for our iniquities" (Isa. 53:5). Other prophets told us even more. From Micah, we learned that the Messiah would be born in Bethlehem (Micah 5:2). From David, we learned that He would die by crucifixion but then rise from the dead (Pss. 22; 16:10). From Daniel, we learned that all of this would take place before the destruction of the second temple, which we know occurred in AD 70 (Dan. 9:25–26).

So once again, we're forced to ask: why all the specific detail, if knowing His identity and believing in Him really isn't so essential?

Seven centuries after Isaiah, we come to the dawn of New Testament times. And when Zacharias describes the future ministry of his son, John the Baptist, he explains that John "will go on before the Lord to prepare His ways; to give to His [Jewish] people the knowledge of salvation by the forgiveness of their sins" (Luke 1:76–77). But if Jews don't need to hear the gospel, then why did God send John the Baptist to give us "the knowledge of salvation" and to point us to "the Lamb of God who takes away the sin of the world" (John 1:29)?

That the prophets announced His coming and implored Jews to look to Him is clear. That Zacharias and John the Baptist pointed us to Him is clear. That Jesus the Messiah proclaimed the gospel to His fellow Jews is clear. That He commanded His followers to do the same is clear. That they obeyed His commandment and followed His example is clear.

There's really no ambiguity about what the biblical record reveals. Even so, many misconceptions and arguments cloud the issue and undermine the need for Jewish evangelism. Let me weigh those arguments and see how they hold up against what the Scriptures teach.

THE MISCONCEPTIONS

CHAPTER 3

"Jews Are Already Saved because They're Natural, Elected, and Chosen"

I've been told . . .

> "The Jews are irrevocably elected. They're the chosen people of God, the natural branches of the olive tree. That means that they already have a proper relationship with God. In essence, they're already saved."

ISRAEL'S ELECTION IS indeed irrevocable, and praise the Lord that it is. If it weren't, then all of us would have grounds for doubting whether we can trust any of God's covenantal promises, including the new covenant promises of the forgiveness of sins and the gift of eternal life. If God can break one covenant, what's to stop Him from breaking them all? Israel's unchanging election stands as a testimony to the fact that even "if we are faithless, He remains faithful, for He cannot deny Himself" (2 Tim. 2:13).

In his letter to the believers in Rome, Paul affirms Israel's election when he asks a rhetorical question and answers with an emphatic cry: "I say then, God has not rejected His people, has He? May it never be! For I too am an Israelite, a descendant of Abraham, of the tribe of Benjamin. God has not rejected His people whom He foreknew" (Rom. 11:1–2). Later in that same chapter, he explains that the people of Israel are the natural branches, while the Gentiles are the wild shoots that have been grafted in (Rom. 11:17–22).

But does *nationally* elected and chosen mean *individually* saved? And does the fact that the Jewish people are the natural branches mean that those very people don't need to receive Yeshua in order to possess a correct *personal* relationship with God? A look at the larger context of the book of Romans, chapters 9 through 11, sheds light on these questions.

God will graft the natural Jewish branches back in, *but only when we abandon our unbelief and believe in Yeshua.*

In his epistle, Paul agonizes so intensely over his people's separation from God that he says, "I could wish that I myself were accursed, separated from Christ for the sake of my brethren, my kinsmen according to the flesh, who are Israelites" (Rom. 9:3–4). And when he prays for his fellow Jews, his "heart's desire and my prayer to God for them is for their salvation" (10:1). In chapter 11, he tells the Roman believers, "Inasmuch then as I am an apostle of Gentiles, I magnify my ministry, if somehow I might move to jealousy my fellow countrymen and save some of them" (11:13–14).

Then, a few verses later, Paul introduces the analogy of the branches (11:17). He speaks of the Jewish people as the natural branches, and he describes the Gentile believers as wild olive shoots that have been grafted in. But does he make the point that Jews are already saved? No, he uses the imagery of the branches in order to explain just the opposite—that even though we're "natural," many of us have been broken off because of our failure to believe. *The analogy of the branches is not given as an assurance of automatic Jewish salvation, but as a warning to Gentile Christians of the dangers of unbelief.* So Paul writes,

> They [the Jews] were broken off for their unbelief, but you stand by your faith. Do not be conceited, but fear; for if God did not spare the natural branches, He will not spare you, either. (Rom. 11:20–21)

There's good news for the Jewish people in the midst of this dire warning to the Gentiles. He promises that, "if they do not continue in their unbelief, [they] will be grafted in, for God is able to graft them in again" (Rom. 11:23). In other words, God will graft the natural Jewish branches back in, *but only when we abandon our unbelief and believe in Yeshua.*

Paul doesn't call us Jews the natural branches as a way of saying that we don't need to be saved. He calls us the natural branches as a way of saying how natural it will be for us to be grafted back in, once we've believed.

> For if you [the Romans] were cut off from what is by
> nature a wild olive tree, and were grafted contrary to
> nature into a cultivated olive tree, how much more will
> these who are the natural branches be grafted into their
> own olive tree? (Rom. 11:24)

Tragically, our failure to believe in Jesus resulted in many of us being broken off. But by God's grace, we can be grafted back in—once we believe in the Lord.

A LIGHT FOR THE NATIONS

So the natural branches are nationally elected and chosen by God, but not automatically saved as individuals. But how can that be? In order to reconcile that seeming paradox, we need to understand what the Hebrew Scriptures mean when they apply the term "chosen" or "elected" to us Jews (e.g., Deut. 7:6; Ps. 33:12; Isa. 44:1).

God chose the Jewish people to perform a particular task: to be a gospel light to the nations of the world. In Isaiah 43, we're told,

> "You are My witnesses" declares the LORD, "and My
> servant whom I have chosen. . . . The people whom
> I formed for Myself will declare My praise."
> (Isa. 43:10, 21)

Seven centuries later, the apostle Peter reiterates that call when writing primarily to his fellow Jewish believers in the Diaspora:

> But you are a chosen race, a royal priesthood, a holy
> nation, a people for God's own possession, so that you
> may proclaim the excellencies of Him who has called
> you out of darkness into His marvelous light.
> (1 Peter 2:9)

Chosen to bear witness and proclaim. What a privilege! But there's a problem. We Jews can't proclaim the gospel until we believe the gospel, and we can't believe the gospel until we hear the gospel, and we can't hear the gospel until someone brings it to us first. No wonder that Paul, the apostle to the Gentiles, always brought the gospel first to his fellow Jews. He understood God's strategy: bring the gospel to the Jewish people so that the Jews can bring the gospel to the world. That's the call. That's why we Jews were chosen.

Satan has a strategy, too: destroy God's gospel messengers. Or, if we can't be destroyed, then drive a wedge between us and our Messiah through the misconduct of Gentiles who claim to belong to Him. And finally, keep the appointed future messengers ignorant of the message by using believers to shield us from the very message we've been chosen to proclaim.

If we understand the call, then we understand why Satan has worked so insidiously, incessantly, and systematically to destroy the people whom God chose. Before Yeshua's first advent, the evil one sought to annihilate us so that he could stop the Scriptures from being written, and so that he could stop the Savior from being born. Since the crucifixion and resurrection, Satan has sought to destroy us so that he could stop the gospel from going out, and so that he could stop the Lord from coming back. Simply put, Jesus is not going to return until Jewish missionaries cover the world with the gospel, and until a repentant, believing Israel cries out, *"Baruch haba b'shem Adonai"*—"Blessed is He who comes in the name of the LORD" (Matt. 23:39). But we can't cry out for the Lord's return until we call on the Lord as our Redeemer.

I've had the privilege of being a missionary to my people for nearly forty years. I've labored in that field for two reasons: because I want to see my people saved, and because I want to see my people fulfill their call. I live and labor for the day when waves of Jewish evangelists will carry the gospel to the nations—especially the nations where we're hated and where so many of us have died. Ironically, the history of our persecutions at the hands of the nations now gives us the platform to proclaim the good news. What a redemption of history! Who can ignore the presence of Jews, openly and unashamedly declaring the message of the cross? Who can turn a blind eye or a deaf ear to the words of the gospel resounding from Jewish lips? Whether we're well received or reviled, the impact is the same. People take note.

But that day of global Jewish proclamation cannot occur unless we first hear the gospel and believe.

Many Christians ardently defend the biblical truth that Jews are still God's chosen people, and I thank God for the stand that those Christians take on our behalf. But many of those same Christians are ignorant of the very purpose for which we were chosen—to proclaim the gospel to the world. As a result, they unwittingly play right into Satan's hands when they oppose the cause of bringing the gospel to the Jews. For, by opposing Jewish evangelism, they're opposing our national salvation, which is the one event that must occur before we can fulfill our missionary call. What an awful twist: some Christians who think of themselves as our most fervent advocates have actually become our most fervent opponents, because they deliberately stand in the way of the fulfillment of the call.

We Jews cannot proclaim the gospel until we believe the gospel. We cannot carry His light to the nations until we carry His light in our hearts.

CHAPTER 4

"God's Covenants with Abraham and Moses Are Good Enough"

I've been told . . .

> "Jews don't need Jesus or His gospel because they have their own way to God. They're saved because of the covenant that God made with Abraham. Or, they're saved so long as they earnestly try to keep the Law."

A TEACHING CALLED dual-covenant theology has become increasingly popular among Christians since the end of the Second World War. Its popularity can be traced to at least two factors: the rise of liberal Protestant theology, and Christian guilt over the church's hostility toward the Jewish people for the past 1,900 years. Ultimately, that hostility culminated in the church's shameful silence over the atrocities committed against the Jewish people by the Nazi regime. In an age when the church wants to cause no further offense, dual-covenant theology offers Christians the opportunity to distance them-selves from a New Testament teaching that we Jews naturally find offensive—the teaching that no one comes to the Father except through the Son. Dual-covenant theology conveniently takes away the offense.

SALVATION BY BIRTH OR REBIRTH?

Essentially, dual-covenant theology argues that the Jewish people have no need for the salvation that we find in the aton-ing death and resurrection of Yeshua, because Jewish people have an adequate saving relationship with God through the covenant that the Lord made with Abraham.

In other words, Jewish people are saved by being descen-dants of the patriarch. We inherit salvation because of our genes. We're saved by birth.

But is this faithful to what the Scriptures teach about the basis of salvation? Is anyone saved by virtue of birth?

John the Baptist contested the notion that the Abrahamic covenant is sufficient for a right relationship with God. He challenged scribes and Pharisees with the words, "do not sup-pose that you can say to yourselves, 'We have Abraham for our father'; for I say to you that from these stones God is able to raise up children to Abraham" (Matt. 3:9).

The apostle Paul refuted the notion of "salvation through the Abrahamic covenant" as well. At Pisidian Antioch, Paul preached to people whom he called "Brethren, sons of Abra-ham's family" (Acts 13:26). He urged them to believe in Yeshua, and he implored them to avoid the peril forewarned by the prophet Habakkuk: "Behold, you scoffers, and marvel, and perish" (Acts 13:41). Why would Paul need to warn these sons of Abraham's family if they were already saved?

Jesus Himself made it clear that Abraham was not saved because of the Abrahamic covenant, but by looking forward in faith and believing in the coming Messiah. "Your father Abraham rejoiced to see My day, and he saw it and was glad" (John 8:56).

> **No one is saved by virtue of birth, but by virtue of *re*birth. That's foundational to the gospel; we must be born *again*.**

The Lord gave many irrevocable promises to Abraham when He entered into the covenant with him as recorded in Genesis 12. He promised the patriarch a land (v. 1), a posterity (v. 2), a great name (v. 2), enduring protection (v. 3), and a blessing that would proceed from Abraham and impact all the families of the earth (v. 3). But He did not promise Abraham's physical descendants an automatic, inherited pardon for sins.

The Abrahamic covenant set the pattern for our salvation by faith alone. "Then he [Abraham] believed in the LORD; and He reckoned it to him as righteousness" (Gen. 15:6). But the pattern is a personal faith, not an inherited covenant. No one is saved by virtue of birth, but by virtue of *re*birth. That's foundational to the gospel; we must be born *again*.

SALVATION BY WORKS
OF THE LAW OR BY FAITH?

Some years ago, I received a telephone call from a Christian woman who all but agonized over the thought that her orthodox Jewish acquaintances faced an eternal separation from the Father unless they placed their faith in the Son. "They're so devout," she said. "Couldn't that devotion be good enough?" I empathized with her distress (and I still do) as I thought of devout, earnest men who ministered to me and to my family when I was a boy: Rabbi Miller, Rabbi Biegeleizen, and others. The last thing I wanted to do was increase her distress. But I had to tell her the truth. So I reminded her that when Jesus said, "'You must be born again,'" He was speaking to a very devout Jewish man—the rabbi Nicodemus (John 3:7). And when Peter cried out at Pentecost, "Repent, and each of you be baptized in the name of Jesus Christ for the forgiveness of your sins" (Acts 2:38), he was also speaking to a group of very devout Jews (2:5).

Is it enough to be devout? Is orthodox devotion and observance sufficient for salvation? Can we be saved by trying to perform the Law? In one sense, the destruction of the second temple in AD 70 renders the whole matter moot, because it's no longer even possible to observe so much of the Law. But even so, let's consider whether Jewish people can be saved by keeping (or by trying to keep) the Law.

Paul, the former student of Gamaliel and the self-declared Hebrew of Hebrews, reminded the Galatians that "by the works of the Law no flesh will be justified" (Gal. 2:16). In fact, he goes on to say that Jesus Himself was born under the Law so that He might redeem those who were likewise under the Law (4:4–5). So, if the Law could redeem us, then why did those of us under the Law need a Redeemer other than the Law itself?

Had salvation been available through the Law, then Paul certainly would have attained it, for he was "found blameless" when measured by that holy and righteous standard (Phil. 3:6). But Paul explains that God did not give us the Law in order to save, but to testify of the Savior. "Therefore the Law has become our tutor to lead us to Christ, so that we may be justified by faith" (Gal. 3:24). And in writing these words, Paul merely reiterated what Yeshua Himself had already explained to some Jewish people who apparently looked to the Law for a correct relationship with the Lord. "You search the Scriptures because you think that in them you have eternal life; it is these that testify about Me" (John 5:39).

When we look at the Law, especially at the sacrifices found in Leviticus, we don't find God's means of salvation; rather we find His message of the gospel. God gave us the Law because He wanted us to understand certain truths about Himself—and about ourselves. He wanted us to understand that we're sinful; that's why we needed to present offerings for our sins. He wanted us to understand that our sins deserve death; that's why the animals had to die. And perhaps most remarkably, He wanted us to understand that in His mercy, He would accept a substitute in our places—a life for a life, a death other than our own.

But the life given in exchange for our own needed to be innocent, like a spotless lamb. Animals, however, can't atone for a human being's sins. As King David explained, "Burnt offering and sin offering You have not required" (Ps. 40:6). But someday, *He* would come—the Messiah. "Behold, I come; in the scroll of the book it is written of me" (Ps. 40:7). He would offer His sinless life as the payment for our transgressions. He would die for our sins and rise from the dead. And if we repented and trusted in what He would do for our sakes rather than trusting in our own righteous conduct, then God would justify us by our faith in *His* work on the cross, not by *our* works of the Law.

The lessons that the sacrifices imparted were summarized by the prophet Isaiah:

> All of us like sheep have gone astray, each of us has turned to his own way; but the Lord has caused the iniquity of us all to fall on Him. He was oppressed and He was afflicted, yet He did not open His mouth; like a lamb that is led to slaughter. (53:6–7)

One of the words used in the Law to speak of the guilt offering is the Hebrew word *asham*. The prophet Isaiah used that very word when he described the sacrifice that the Messiah would make as the payment for our transgressions.

> If He would render Himself as a guilt offering [*asham*], He will see His offspring, He will prolong His days . . . By His knowledge the Righteous One, My Servant, will justify the many, as He will bear their iniquities. (53:10–11)

The sacrifices of the Law didn't save. They pointed us to the Savior. How eloquently did the prophet Isaiah encapsulate this purpose of the Law when he described Yeshua as our *asham*. And how concisely did the last of the Old Testament–style prophets, John the Baptist, direct us to the One who *is* our *asham*: "Behold, the lamb of God who takes away the sin of the world!" (John 1:29).

Like Abraham and Moses, my ancestors were saved if they looked forward in faith to the Lamb of God who would die for their sins and rise from the dead. Today, whether Jewish or not, we are saved when we look back in faith to the Lamb of God who died for our sins and then rose from the dead. But there has always been only one Lamb. There has always been only one way. And Jesus said, "I am the way, and the truth, and the life; no one comes to the Father but through Me" (John 14:6).

CHAPTER 5

"Jews Will Be Judged Only According to the Light That They've Received"

I've been told . . .

> "God certainly won't judge a Jewish person who hasn't had the opportunity to hear the good news. God will only judge people according to the light that they've received."

THE QUESTION OF the eternal destiny of those who have never heard the gospel deals with two subjects that make all of us uncomfortable: *accountability* and *judgment*. The idea that "God won't judge a person who hasn't heard" reminds us that God is a judge. And the idea that "God will call people into account only according to the light that we've received" reminds us that we will be held accountable. We don't like that very much.

But at the same time, the notion that God will judge only according to the received light seems to soften this matter of accountability quite a bit. The argument suggests the promise of an escape, or the existence of an exemption clause. That's a comforting thought, both for those who haven't yet believed, and for those of us who worry about friends and loved ones, Jewish and otherwise, who haven't yet heard. But if God judges people only according to the light that they've received, we need to ask, "What's the light that we Jews have received? What's the standard by which we'll be judged?"

Jesus Himself gave us the answer, but unfortunately, it's not an easy answer to hear. He said,

> "Do not think that I will accuse you before the Father; the one who accuses you is Moses, in whom you have set your hope. For if you believed Moses, you would believe Me, for he wrote about Me." (John 5:45–46)

These words hardly seem comforting. If anything, they're unsettling. According to Yeshua, even if we Jews never hear the gospel, we'll be held accountable for failing to find "Him of whom Moses in the Law and also the Prophets wrote" (John 1:45).

The hard truth that we must face is this: we *have* been given light. *All* of us. Paul explains that *everyone*—Jews and non-Jews alike—will be held accountable for failing to believe, if for no other reason than

> that which is known about God is evident within them; for God made it evident to them. For since the creation of the world His invisible attributes, His eternal power and divine nature, have been clearly seen,

being understood through what has been made, so that they are without excuse. (Rom. 1:19–20)

It's a sobering and difficult thought, but we have to wrestle with it all the same. If all humanity will be held accountable for failing to grasp the reality of God's attributes, power, and nature simply from the testimony of His creation, how much more will we Jews be held accountable for failing to grasp His identity as revealed in the Law, the Prophets, and the Writings?

COMING TO THE LIGHT

Ironically, many Jewish people haven't ever really examined the Scriptures that God entrusted to us. We're "people of the Book," but we haven't actually looked into the Book to see what it has to say. This means that though we're still accountable, we can't honestly be accused of "rejecting" what we haven't been told. There's a glimmer of hope and encouragement in this. For, not infrequently, when we do encounter the Messiah in our Jewish Scriptures—when we're shown the Light—our initial surprise is followed by a desire to know more, and ultimately, by a willingness to believe.

I remember a time when a colleague of mine, Julia, visited a young woman named Miriam.

"Do you have a copy of the Hebrew Scriptures?" Julia asked.

Miriam found a copy in her bookcase and took it down.

"Let me show you something," Julia said. She opened the Bible to Isaiah 53 while explaining that the passage was a prophecy that had been penned around 700 BC. Then she placed the Bible back into Miriam's hands and asked her to read. Miriam's eyes literally grew wide as she read from her own Bible the description of the Servant of the Lord who dies as an atonement for our sins.

"Does this sound like anyone you've ever heard about?" Julia asked.

"It sounds like Jesus." She looked down at her Bible, reread the passage, and asked, "Why don't the rabbis believe this?"

"Actually, that's the wrong question," Julia answered warmly. "The *right* question is, 'Why don't *you* believe this?'"

Miriam thought for another moment. Then she said, "I do."

Isaiah wrote, "Arise, shine; for your light has come" (Isa. 60:1). Sometimes, all we need is a nudge in the direction of our Light.

WHAT ABOUT THOSE
WHO'VE NEVER HEARD?

A number of years ago, another colleague named Laurie discussed the claims of the Lord with a young Jewish woman as they sat in an outdoor café. With the Scriptures opened on the table before them, Laurie introduced the young woman, Sandra, to some of the key messianic passages in the Hebrew Scriptures like Micah 5:2 (5:1 Heb.), Psalm 22, and of course, Isaiah 53. Apparently, Sandra could see the truth, because for several moments, she sat very still, silently weighing the matter in her heart. Then, she shifted abruptly in her chair and demanded to know, "But what about all the people who've never had the chance to hear? Is God going to hold them accountable, even if they've never heard?"

Laurie refocused the question where it needed to be. "We're not talking about people who haven't heard," she answered softly. "We're talking about you and me. And you and I *have* heard."

The truth is that we *have* heard and we *have* been told—whether we're Jewish or not. David wrote, "The heavens are telling of the glory of God; and their expanse is declaring the work of His hands" (Ps. 19:1). The creation alone alerts us to the fact that the Creator is real. Is that enough

God promises that if we respond to the very basic revelation that He exists with a desire to know more, then He will lead us to the specific revelation of the Messiah and His gospel.

to make us right with God? No, but God promises that if we respond to the very basic revelation that He exists with a desire to know more, then He will lead us to the specific revelation of the Messiah and His gospel, and He will bring us to Himself. "You will seek Me and find Me," God promises, "when you search for Me with all your heart. I will be found by you" (Jer. 29:13–14).

We see this principle in action in the life of the Roman centurion Cornelius. The man was an alien to the household of Israel. But he knew that God was real, and he wanted to know who He was. So he prayed, and he performed good deeds. How did God reward him? He didn't say, "Well done, Cornelius. That's good enough." He rewarded Cornelius's desire to know Him by sending him the apostle Peter, who told Cornelius the good news.

God did the same for the Ethiopian eunuch whom we encounter in Acts 8. The Lord pulled the disciple Philip away from what seems to have been a full-blown revival in Samaria so that he could bring the eunuch's spiritual search to an end.

If the Lord honored the desires of a Roman centurion who wanted to worship Israel's God, and if the Lord answered the longings of an Ethiopian eunuch who wanted to understand what he read in the Jewish Scriptures, will He do anything less for the daughter or son of Israel who has heeded the announcements found in Moses and the prophets and wants to know where those announcements lead?

SOMEONE MORE, SOMETHING NEW

In Deuteronomy we read that God will send another prophet like Moses: "The LORD your God will raise up for you a prophet like me [Moses] from among you, from your countrymen, you shall listen to him" (18:15). Not only will He raise up another prophet like Moses, but He will also usher in a new covenant that surpasses the one that Moses ushered in: "'days are coming,' declares the LORD, 'when I will make a new covenant with the house of Israel and with the house of Judah, not like the covenant which I made with their fathers in the day I took them by the hand to bring them out of the land of Egypt'" (Jer. 31:31–32). What's one of the crowning achievements and a major difference between this new covenant and the one enacted when He brought the Israelites out of Egypt? God says that under the new covenant, "I will forgive their iniquity, and their sin I will remember no more" (Jer. 31:34).

Moses and the prophets told us that we should be expecting Someone else and that we should be awaiting something new. If we'd paid closer attention to Moses and the prophets, then we would have been looking for Someone and something more. But sadly, so many of us didn't, and so many of us don't—at least, not until someone like Philip climbs into our chariot and asks, "Do you understand what you are reading?" Not until someone like Peter explains.

EVEN IN THE DARKEST DAYS

There's no region where God has failed to shed his light, even during the darkest days of our recent past—during the Shoah, or Holocaust, when six million of us died. Though "hard" statistics elude us, some people estimate that as many as sixty thousand Jewish believers in Jesus went to the death camps with the rest of our people. And there were thousands of Gentile Christians who chose to identify with us in our tribulation and perish with us in the camps. If only a fraction of those Jewish and non-Jewish believers were vocal, then a significant gospel testimony existed even in places like Auschwitz, Treblinka, and Sobibor. If they weren't silent, then others had a chance to hear.

The problem doesn't lie with a God who refuses to shed His light. The problem lies with our unbelieving hearts that refuse to receive His light.

There are no spiritual black holes that God cannot or will not penetrate with His light. The problem doesn't lie with a God who refuses to shed His light. The problem lies with our unbelieving hearts that refuse to receive His light. And the problem lies with believers who refuse to bear His light to those who are looking for a way out of the dark.

We will indeed be judged according to the light that we've

received. By God's grace, and because He wants to be known, that illumination shines bright! But the fact that we'll be judged only "according to the light" isn't an exemption clause for Jewish people or for anyone else. It's a call to action that believers need to heed for the sake of their unsaved family and friends.

We Jews need people who will tell us that the Light of Life has come. We need people like Philip who will climb into the chariot and ask if we understand what we read. We need people like Peter who will cross the cultural threshold and tell us the information that we lack. We need people to say, "Come, house of Jacob, and let us walk in the light of the LORD" (Isa. 2:5).

CHAPTER 6

"Jesus Is Israel's *Only* but *Anonymous* Savior"

I've been told . . .

> "Jewish people don't need to know the Savior's identity in order to be saved. Yes, Jesus is the only Savior, and yes, there's salvation in no other name. But Jewish people don't need to know that right away. They'll know who He is and what He's done for them when they see Him face-to-face."

THERE ARE A NUMBER of problems with the contention that Jesus can be an anonymous Savior of us Jews. The most obvious problem is that it contradicts the clear teaching of Scripture. In the first chapter of the gospel of John, a distinction is made between the Jewish people who received Him and those who did not. We're told that, "He came to His own, and those who were His own did not receive Him. But as many as received Him, to them He gave the right to become children of God, even to those who believe in His name" (John 1:11–12).

Certainly, believing in His name involves knowing who He is. It's those Jewish people who knew Him and believed in His name who became the children of God. Later in that same gospel, we read of the time when Yeshua told a group of Pharisees, "You know neither Me nor My Father; if you knew Me, you would know My Father also" (John 8:19). In other words, in order to know the Father, these Pharisees needed to know the identity of the Son. What was true for my ancestors is true for us today.

The notion of an anonymous savior for us Jews raises the question, "Does *anyone* really need to know who Jesus is in order to be saved?" If Jesus can be an anonymous Savior for the Jewish people, then why can't He be an anonymous Savior for the world? Ultimately, that line of reasoning leads us to the conclusion that no one needs to proclaim, no one needs to hear, and no one needs to believe in His name in order to be saved.

ONCE, AT A SEMINARY

In the early 1980s, I accompanied Moishe Rosen, the founder of Jews for Jesus, when he called on the president of a seminary in the States. Moishe had heard that the president might be wavering in his commitment to the belief that Yeshua is the only way of salvation. But rather than believe the rumor, Moishe decided to find out for himself by paying the president a visit, and he invited me to come along.

We sat in the president's office, drank some coffee, and ate pretzels that the secretary had set out. In keeping with professional courtesy, the president inquired about our missionary work, and after giving a quick update, Moishe asked in turn how things were going at the school. Then Moishe asked the question that he'd flown down to ask. "So do you believe that Jesus is the only Savior for Jews and non-Jews alike?"

The president must have been expecting the question, because he didn't hesitate at all before giving his reply. "Absolutely," he said.

That seemed to settle the matter. I remember sitting there, hoping that we might start talking about some other things, because the coffee was good, and I wanted to stay for a second cup.

Then Moishe asked a follow-up question that I never would have thought to ask. "But do you believe that a Jewish person needs to *know* that it's Jesus who saves him?"

The president balked. "Well," he said, "that's more difficult to answer."

As it turned out, there was time for a second cup, after all.

CREATED TO KNOW HIM IN A PERSONAL WAY

The notion that God is content to be an anonymous Savior runs contrary to everything that the Bible teaches us about the very character and conduct of God. He created us so that we might enjoy an intimate relationship with Him. He corrects us when we rebel. He seeks us when we're lost. He cries out to us over and over again through the voices of the prophets, calling us to return. Ultimately, He sent His only begotten Son to reveal Himself fully, and to bring us back to Him. Why would God do all of that if He were content to remain unknown?

The word *revelation* reminds us that the God of the Bible is not a God who shrouds Himself in secrecy, but who discloses who He is, what He's done, and what we need to know in order to be saved.

Time after time, we encounter a telltale statement in Moses and the prophets. God tells us that He's acted, or that He's going to act, specifically so that we "will know that I am the LORD" (e.g., Ex. 6:7; Deut. 29:6; Isa. 49:23; Ezek. 6:7). Even the word *revelation* reminds us that the God of the Bible is not a God who shrouds Himself in secrecy, but who discloses who He is, what He's done, and what we need to know in order to be saved.

Granted, we can't know or understand everything about Him. He's the infinite Creator; we're His finite creatures. He's holy and perfect; we're broken and corrupt. But that doesn't alter the fact that He commands and even implores us to seek Him, to find Him and to know Him in an intimate way.

> "I have not spoken in secret, in some dark land; I did not say to the offspring of Jacob, 'Seek Me in a waste place.'" (Isa. 45:19)

> Seek the LORD while He may be found; call upon Him while He is near. (Isa. 55:6)

> "You will seek Me and find Me, when you search for Me with all your heart. I will be found by you." (Jer. 29:13–14)

These are not the words of a God who will settle for obscurity and anonymity. Rather, these are the words of a God who longs to be known and loved.

FULFILLING THE GREATEST COMMANDMENT

In the gospel of Mark, we read about an encounter between Yeshua and a scribe who asked the Lord, "What commandment is the foremost of all?" (Mark 12:28). Yeshua answered by quoting the very first verse that many of us Jews learn as children, and the very last verse we utter if we're lucid just before we die. "Hear, O Israel! The LORD is our God, the LORD is one!" Then He continued, "You shall love the LORD your God with all your heart and with all your soul and with all your might" (Deut. 6:4–5).

Yeshua's reply raises some challenging questions: If the greatest commandment is to love the Lord wholeheartedly, how can we love Him if we don't know who He is? How can we love a Lord whose name is a mystery, and whose deeds on our behalf have never been explained?

HEEDING THE PROPHET LIKE MOSES

As I mentioned before, in Deuteronomy 18, we read about a prophet like Moses whom God promises to send, and whom God commands us to heed:

> I will raise up a prophet from among their countrymen like you [Moses], and I will put my words in his mouth . . . It shall come about that whoever will not listen to My words which he shall speak in My name, I Myself will require it of him." (Deut. 18:18–19)

As believers in Yeshua, we know that this prophet like Moses is Jesus (Acts 3:22; 7:37). He is the One whom God promised to send, and He is the One whom God commanded us to heed. But how can we heed Him if we don't know who He is? How can we listen to His words and obey His voice if we don't know what He's said?

SAVED TO SERVE OUR REDEEMER AND LORD

Yeshua is not just our Savior. He's our Redeemer and Lord. "Thus says the LORD, the King of Israel and his Redeemer, the LORD of hosts . . . I, the LORD, am your Savior and your Redeemer, the Mighty One of Jacob" (Isa. 44:6; 60:16).

An anonymous savior might be content to remain an unknown benefactor who rescues us from afar with no further expectations from the people whom he's saved. But a Redeemer/Lord requires and expects so much more.

The word "redemption" speaks of a transaction in which the redeemed individual has been bought. That individual is not free; he or she is owned. As a result, there are obligations in the contractual, covenantal relationship. The Redeemer expects the redeemed to know what He promises, and to know what He requires. In the same way, the title "Lord" speaks of a relationship between a master and a servant, where the one who has been bought now lives to obey the Lord's words and fulfill His will.

But how can we know what our Redeemer requires, and how can we fulfill our Lord's will if we don't know who He is and what He wants us to do?

IGNORANT WORSHIP OF AN UNKNOWN GOD

In Acts 17, we read about the time when the apostle Paul commented on the Athenians' deference to a god they didn't know.

> "Men of Athens, I observe that you are very religious in all respects. For while I was passing through and examining the objects of your worship, I also found an altar with this inscription, 'To an unknown god.' Therefore what you worship in ignorance, this I proclaim to you." (Acts 17:22–23)

If God wanted to be known to the Gentile nations, are we to understand that He doesn't care if He remains anonymous to the Jewish nation that He called?

No, He cares. And He wants us to know precisely who He is so that we may love Him and serve Him with all our heart, soul, mind, and strength. "Then you will know that I, the LORD, am your Savior and your Redeemer, the Mighty One of Jacob" (Isa. 60:16).

CHAPTER 7

"Jewish People Can't Believe because They Are Hardened, Blind, and Veiled from Seeing the Truth"

I've been told . . .

> "There's no point in trying to evangelize the Jewish people at this time, because there's a veil over their minds and hearts."

A MISCONCEPTION AMONG some Christians is that the Jewish people have a veil over our eyes that blinds us from seeing the truth about Jesus at this time. According to the argument, we're so hardened that we simply can't believe—at least, not yet, not now. And that's why this is the time of the *Gentiles*—the time for Gentiles to hear and believe. But once the time of the Gentiles is completed, then the veil will be lifted, the hardness will be gone, and the Jewish people will be able to believe.

But is that correct? Exactly what does Paul say about this "veil?"

> But their [the Jewish people's] minds were hardened; for until this very day at the reading of the old covenant the same veil remains unlifted, because it is removed in Christ. But to this day whenever Moses is read, a veil lies over their heart; but whenever a person turns to the Lord, the veil is taken away. (2 Cor. 3:14–16)

At first glance, it might seem as though Paul is saying that a veil prevents us from understanding the gospel and coming to faith. But is that actually what the apostle is saying? Thankfully, no! According to these verses, Paul is saying that a veil prevents us Jews from understanding *the Law of Moses*, not from understanding the good news. "For until this very day, at the reading of the *old covenant* the same veil remains unlifted . . . But to this day whenever *Moses* is read, a veil lies over their heart."

Our minds and hearts are not veiled from understanding the gospel. Rather, our minds and hearts are veiled from understanding what Moses has to say—specifically, what Moses has to say about Yeshua. No wonder, then, that we can read the weekly portion from Moses and the prophets every Saturday in our synagogues, but fail to see the One of whom Moses and the prophets wrote. But that veil is removed, Paul says, once a Jewish person comes to faith in the Lord. That veil, Paul says in the verses above, "is removed in Christ."

Implicit in Paul's whole argument is the notion that Jewish

people *can* turn to the Lord when the gospel is presented. And then, once we believe, the veil is lifted, and the old covenant makes sense.

A PARTIAL HARDENING, NOT TOTAL

As for Israel's hardened state, does Paul actually say that at the present time, Israel is hardened and cannot believe? We might be tempted to come to that mistaken conclusion if we failed to take into account *everything* that Paul tells us about this "hardening." In Romans 11:25, he qualifies the hardening by saying "a *partial* hardening has happened to Israel until the fullness of the Gentiles has come in" (Rom. 11:25).

The crucial word that holds the key to understanding Paul's intent is *partial.* Paul does not say that at the present time Israel is so hardened that she cannot believe, nor does he say that because of that hardheartedness, the gospel should only be proclaimed to the Gentiles in this day and age. Rather, he explains that a *partial* hardening has happened to Israel. Partial, not complete. That means that whereas many—perhaps even most—Jewish people will not come to faith at the present time because of the hardness of our hearts, many others *will* come to faith, if only we're given the chance to hear the good news and given the opportunity to respond.

THE TIME OF THE
GENTILES DOESN'T EXCLUDE JEWS

And what about this "time of the Gentiles"? Does "time of the Gentiles" mean that it's *only* the time of the Gentiles?

Obviously not, or else Paul wouldn't have expended so much of that time in bringing the gospel to his fellow Jews. Paul knew that even during this "time of the Gentiles," there would always be a significant number of his countrymen who were ready to believe. Paul knew that there would always be a believing, faithful remnant. That remnant existed in Elijah's day, that remnant existed in Paul's day, and that remnant exists today. The proof of what I'm saying should be obvious enough: a member of that present-day remnant is writing these very words to you *now*.

So even though the greater number of Jewish people will come to faith when the time of the Gentiles draws to a close, there still exists at this present time a remnant according to God's gracious choice, waiting to hear and ready to believe.

CHAPTER 8

"All Israel Will Be Saved . . . Eventually"

I've been told . . .

> "Jewish evangelism is premature, because all Jewish people will be saved anyway, when the Lord returns. After all, Paul himself assured us that 'all Israel will be saved' (Rom. 11:26). And, we learn from Zechariah 12:10 that this national repentance will occur after Jesus has come back, when the Jewish people look on Him whom they have pierced. Not only will this national salvation cover all the Jewish people at that time, but that phrase 'all Israel' actually refers to all Jewish people, past and present, living or dead. And it all occurs after Jesus has come back."

PAUL DOES INDEED tell us that all Israel will be saved (Rom. 11:26). There's no question about that. But he also tells us *how* all Israel will be saved: only by calling on the name of the Lord. In fact, he explains that the need to call exclusively on the name of the Lord is a universal truth: "For there is no distinction between Jew and Greek; for the same Lord is Lord of all, abounding in riches for all who call on Him; for 'Whoever will call on the name of the Lord will be saved'" (Rom. 10:12–13).

But right after stating that there is only one Lord for all, and that salvation is available only by calling on His name, Paul then raises a series of challenging questions: "How then will they call on Him in whom they have not believed? And how will they believe in Him whom they have not heard?" (Rom. 10:14).

So, all people—Jews and Gentiles—need to hear in order to believe, and they need to believe in order to call, and they need to call on the name of the Lord in order to be saved. And in order for any of that to happen, somebody has to carry the gospel message, not just to the Gentiles, but to the Jews. That's why Paul continues with the questions: "And how will they hear without a preacher? How will they preach unless they are sent?" (Rom. 10:14–15).

While Romans 11:26 tells us the *fact* that all Israel will be saved, Romans 10:12–15 tells us the *manner* in which all Israel will be saved—by hearing the gospel message, believing unto repentance, and calling on the name of the Lord.

The words of Romans 11 are our comfort—all Israel will be saved. But the words of Romans 10 are our commission— we must tell the Jewish people about Jesus so they may hear, believe, call, and be saved. Though the commission may be hard to bear, Paul ends the passage with a wonderful promise for those who are willing to go. "How beautiful are the feet of those who bring good news of good things!" (Rom. 10:15).

SO WHAT'S THE RUSH?

But since all Israel will be saved anyway, can't we bypass the Jews for now? Won't they call on Him when they look on Him? And won't they look on Him when He returns?

I know a lovely Jewish man named Aaron (not his real name). At the time of this writing, Aaron is in his nineties. He still has a clear mind. He still has a quick wit. And he still has a nonbelieving heart when it comes to Jesus. Whenever I ask him how he's doing, he smiles and says, "Well, I'm old, but I'm alive, and that beats the alternative."

Some Christians would actually disagree. Essentially, they'd argue that whether or not Aaron ever believes in the Lord or lives to see Jesus return, he has nothing to fear. "Either Aaron will come to faith after looking on Him when He returns, or he will be saved after death, even if he dies in unbelief."

But is that what Paul meant when he said, "All Israel will be saved"? And is that what the prophet Zechariah foretold when he declared, "they will look on Me whom they have pierced"?

REPENTANCE *BEFORE* HE RETURNS

What does Zechariah 12:10 actually say?

> I will pour out on the house of David and on the inhabitants of Jerusalem, the Spirit of grace and of supplication, so that they will look on Me whom they have pierced; and they will mourn for Him, as one mourns for an only son.

I've been told that to "look on Me" must mean that Jews will see Him after He returns. And so, that's the moment when all of us will repent—*after* He returns. But there are at least three reasons why that argument doesn't hold up. The first and most important reason is this: that's not what the passage in Zechariah says.

Zechariah 12:10 begins by explaining that God will *first* pour out a twofold spirit upon us Jews: His spirit of grace, and then His spirit of supplication. This means that by His Spirit, the Lord will first pour out His grace—the very grace that enables any of us to believe and be saved. And by His grace, He will provoke us to make supplication, which means that He will move us to repent. Only then, *after* making supplication and repenting, will we look on Him whom we have pierced. That's what the text says. That's what the order of the words in the verse declares.

In other words, the text does *not* say that we'll look on Him after His return, recognize Him as the One we've pierced, and then repent. Rather, the sequence of the text explains that the act of looking on Him happens *after* we make supplication and repent!

And isn't this precisely how Jesus told us it would happen? "For I say to you, from now on you will not see Me until you say, 'Blessed is He who comes in the name of the LORD!'"

(Matt. 23:39). Centuries before Yeshua's first coming, God's Spirit foretold the same sequence of events through the prophet Hosea: "I will go away and return to My place until they acknowledge their guilt and seek My face" (Hos. 5:15).

Jesus comes back only *after* we acknowledge Him as the blessed One who comes in the name of the Lord. He comes back only *after* we have made supplication and repented for having spurned Him, the One whom we pierced.

But in order to repent for having spurned Him, we have to have heard about what He did on our behalf. We have to hear the message of the gospel.

The words of Zechariah 12:10 don't give us the license to bypass or postpone bringing the gospel to the Jewish people. The words of this verse should actually motivate us to share the gospel with our Jewish friends and relatives even more fervently, in anticipation of the day when the prophecy will come to pass.

THE URGENCY OF JESUS AND HIS DISCIPLES

There's a second reason that contradicts the notion that Zechariah 12:10 allows us to postpone or bypass Jewish evangelism today: neither the Lord nor His apostles held to that mistaken point of view. Rather, they believed that present-day Jewish evangelism was very much in order. How do we know? Because if they *had* believed the notion that Zechariah 12:10 provides a license for bypassing or postponing Jewish evangelism, then neither Yeshua nor His first followers would have devoted so much time, energy, and heartfelt passion to evangelizing the Jewish people of their day.

A SECOND CHANCE?

Finally, we should ask ourselves, "What about the Jewish people who are living now and who will not be alive whenever that moment of national repentance occurs? What about my friend Aaron, who's not likely to see the Lord's return unless He returns in the very near future? Are Aaron and all the rest of the Jewish people exempt from believing *now*? Will they be given a second chance after Yeshua comes back? Will they have another opportunity to repent, after dying? Not according to the Scriptures. The Holy Spirit was speaking initially to Jewish people when He said through the writer of the book of Hebrews, "it is appointed for men to die once and after this comes judgment" (Heb. 9:27). And through the prophet Daniel, He declared, "Many of those who sleep in the dust of the ground will awake, these to everlasting life, but the others to disgrace and everlasting contempt" (Dan. 12:2). There's no second chance for Jews, or for anyone else, after death.

WILL ALL ISRAEL BE SAVED?

But doesn't Paul assure us under the inspiration of the Holy Spirit that all Israel will be saved? Yes, he does. But "all Israel" doesn't refer to all Jewish people, whether living or dead, past or present. There's a tragic and extremely disquieting biblical truth that we have to face if we want to understand Paul's meaning when he writes, "all Israel will be saved." The "all Israel" refers to the one-third of us Jews who will survive the most horrific time that awaits the Jewish people.

"It will come about in all the land," declares the LORD, "that two parts in it will be cut off and perish; but the third will be left in it. And I will bring the third part through the fire, refine them as silver is refined, and test them as gold is tested. They will call on My name, and I will answer them; I will say, 'They are My people,' and they will say, 'The LORD is my God.'" (Zech. 13:8–9)

It's brutally hard to envision a future catastrophe that awaits the nation, even greater than what befell us during the nightmare of the Holocaust. But that's what God tells us through Zechariah. Two-thirds of us will perish at the hands of our enemies. But the third that remains will be redeemed by the Lord. And thus, all Israel will be saved.

When the Lord returns, the Israel He defends will be the Israel that has repented and whom He has already spiritually redeemed. He will rescue us because we will have repented and looked to Him, the One whom we have pierced. And what a wonderful rescue and vindication of our people it will be.

And in that day living waters will flow out of Jerusalem. . . . And the LORD will be king over all the earth; in that day the LORD will be the only one, and His name the only one. . . . Then it will come about that any who are left of all the nations that went against Jerusalem will go up from year to year to worship the King, the LORD of hosts, and to celebrate the Feast of Booths. (Zech. 14:8, 9, 16)

A DAY OF JOY FOR SOME,
JUDGMENT FOR OTHERS

Those of us who know and love the Lord eagerly long for His return. For us, it will be a day of rejoicing. So perhaps it's easy to forget that for those who've failed to believe before His return, that time of His second coming won't be a day of rejoicing, but a day of reckoning and unparalleled distress. When Jesus returns, He will usher in the fearful and terrible day of the Lord. The descriptions of that event should cause us to agonize—just as the prophets agonized—for anyone who may be found in unbelief when He returns:

> Alas for the day! For the day of the Lord is near, and it will come as destruction from the Almighty. . . . Blow a trumpet in Zion, and sound an alarm on My holy mountain! Let all the inhabitants of the land tremble, for the day of the Lord is coming; surely, it is near, a day of darkness and gloom, a day of clouds and thick darkness. (Joel 1:15; 2:1–2)

> Wail, for the day of the Lord is near! It will come as destruction from the Almighty. Therefore all hands will fall limp, and every man's heart will melt. They will be terrified, pains and anguish will take hold of them; they will writhe like a woman in labor, they will look at one another in astonishment, their faces aflame. Behold, the day of the Lord is coming, cruel, with fury and burning anger, to make the land a desolation; and He will exterminate its sinners from it. (Isa. 13:6–9)

This will not be a day of salvation for those who haven't heard or for those who have refused to believe. This will be a day of accountability. Jesus is not coming back to save those who haven't yet believed. He's coming back to judge. He's coming back as the Lion of Judah.

I remember a time when when my friend Steve Cohen and I visited a rabbi who had been a boyhood acquaintance of Steve's. The rabbi welcomed us graciously, and extended us the courtesy of listening to what Steve wanted to say. After Steve had finished, the rabbi shrugged politely and dismissed the matter with these words: "When Messiah comes, and if He turns out to be your Jesus, then I'll believe." I remember Steve's loving but ardent reply: "After Jesus comes back, it'll be too late."

Yes, when the Lord returns, every knee will bow and every tongue will confess that Yeshua is Lord. That day will mark the end of a victorious battle, when Jesus defends repentant and spiritually redeemed Israel against all her enemies. And at the end of that battle, all will acknowledge what cannot be denied any longer—that He is the Lord. Some will declare that truth with the jubilation that rings in the voices of those who have been rescued from all-but-certain destruction. Others, however, will acknowledge that Jesus is Lord in heart-wrenching anguish for having failed to believe. And while many will bow the knee in blessing and loving adoration, others will bend the knee in defeat as vanquished foes.

Today is not yet the day of the Lord. Today is still the day of salvation, and the proclamation of the gospel to all people—Jews and non-Jews alike—must not be postponed, for

God is *now* declaring to men that all people everywhere should repent, because He has fixed a day in which He will judge the world in righteousness through a Man whom He has appointed, having furnished proof to all men by raising Him from the dead. (Acts 17:30–31)

Do the words "they will look on Me" give us license to bypass or postpone Jewish evangelism? Do the words "all Israel will be saved" dismiss the need for bringing the gospel to the Jews? Not at all! Those words should compel us to proclaim with greater urgency, even now "all the more as you see the day [of the Lord] drawing near" (Heb. 10:25); even now, so long as this "day of salvation" remains.

CHAPTER 9

"Jesus Is Just for the Gentiles"

I've been told . . .

> "Jewish evangelism isn't necessary because Jesus is just a light to Gentiles; He's not the Messiah of the Jews. In fact, following His resurrection, Jesus never even commanded the apostles and disciples to proclaim the gospel to the Jews. The commandment to go into all the world and to make disciples of the nations was just that—a directive to bring the good news to the Gentile nations of the world, not to remain in Israel, preaching to the Jews."

AT FIRST GLANCE, there's something very heartwarming and appealing in the notion that Jesus is God's saving light for the nations, even if He isn't the Messiah of the Jews. The idea reminds us of the fact that God's compassion is by no means limited to the well-being of Israel; His concern extends to all humanity. In His love and grace, God has provided a light to the Gentiles so that the nations will not be left to grope hopelessly in the dark—forsaken, despairing, and lost. Rather,

> There will be no more gloom for her who was in anguish . . . Galilee of the Gentiles . . . The people who walk in darkness will see a great light; those who live in a dark land, the light will shine on them. (Isa. 9:1–2)

According to this argument, Jesus is the Father's provision for the Gentiles, not for the Jews. He's the Savior of the nations, so that God's salvation "may reach to the end of the earth" (Isa. 49:6). What we often call the Great Commission was God's commandment to take the good news only to the nations. That's why Jesus said, "Go into all the *world*" (Mark 16:15) and "make disciples of all the *nations*" (Matt. 28:19).

But there are a number of weaknesses to the argument that God's mandate to "go into all the world" excludes the Jewish people. In the first place, the argument overlooks the normal, inclusive way that the Bible often uses certain words. For example, in Exodus 4:22, God says, "Israel is My son, My firstborn." The title is an expression that describes Israel's election by God, the nation's "chosen-ness." The text literally says "son," but that doesn't mean that women are excluded. Are only Israel's males among the chosen people of God? No, certainly not.

Similarly, in the first chapter of the book of Isaiah, God voices His heartbreak over our national disobedience by declaring, "My people do not understand. Alas, sinful nation . . . *sons* who act corruptly" (Isa. 1:3, 4). Commonsense and context tell us that "sons" includes all people, not just males.

This inclusive use of certain words in the Hebrew Scriptures is carried over in the New Testament as well. For example, 1 Timothy 2:5 tells us that there is "one mediator between God and men, the man Christ Jesus." Here again, "men" means all people, including women and children.

Then there's the problem presented by the disciples' understanding of Yeshua's words. Did they think that Yeshua was telling them to proclaim the gospel only to non-Jews? No, not at all. As the body of Messiah expanded geographically, beyond the borders of ancient Israel, Jewish people were always included among the nations or nationalities that the missionaries sought to reach. Even when the apostle Paul declared in Corinth, "we are turning to the Gentiles" (Acts 13:46), he still continued to proclaim the gospel "to the Jew first" whenever he moved on to start his work in a new city.

But perhaps the strongest challenge to the idea that "all the world" and "all the nations" excludes us Jews is found in the words of Jesus Himself. Shortly before His ascension, He told His disciples, "you shall be My witnesses both in Jerusalem, and in all Judea and Samaria, and even to the remotest part of the earth" (Acts 1:8). Had He meant to limit their gospel proclamation just to non-Jews, then why didn't He leave very Jewish Jerusalem and Judea out of the picture? To avoid confusion, why didn't He say, "you shall be My witnesses just to the *Gentiles* of Jerusalem and Judea"?

The people of Israel certainly constitute one of the nations of the world. And as the apostles carried the gospel to the nations, they never excluded the Jewish people from their evangelistic activity. I suspect that a person would have to be pre-committed against Jewish evangelism in order to believe that exclusion was the intention behind Yeshua's words.

JESUS POINTED THE
JEWISH PEOPLE TO HIMSELF

But how can Yeshua merely be a light to the Gentiles without being a light to His fellow Jews? How can He accomplish only a turning to God for the Gentiles, while remaining unnecessary for us Jews? The argument goes like this: In His role as the light to the nations, Jesus calls for the Gentiles to turn away from their false gods by looking *up* to Him. And by looking up toward Jesus, they're actually looking beyond the man Jesus, toward the God of Israel. This is how Jesus serves as God's light of salvation for the nations.

But we Jews are already looking to God. So, if we mistakenly turn our faces toward Jesus, then we're actually averting our faces from God in order to focus on a man.

What does this argument teach about Jesus and the Gentiles? It teaches that He's something good for the Gentiles, because He causes them to turn their faces upward toward God. But what does this same argument imply about Jesus when it comes to the Jews? It implies that He's a diversion who causes us to turn our faces away from God. That would be a bad enough statement about the Lord. But the argument actually implies something much worse. It implies that He is a deliberate deceiver of Jews.

It's clear in the gospel accounts that Jesus deliberately called the Jewish people to look to Him. For example, when

He declared in the temple courts, "If anyone is thirsty, let him come to Me and drink" (John 7:37), He was calling out to us Jews. When He uttered the words, "How often I wanted to gather your children together, the way a hen gathers her chicks under her wings" (Matt. 23:37), He was lamenting over us Jews. And when He warned, "unless you eat the flesh of the Son of Man and drink His blood, you have no life in yourselves" (John 6:53), He was warning us Jews. In these three instances (and in many more), Jesus specifically implored Jewish people to turn and look to Him. Are we supposed to believe that Yeshua, the Holy One of God, deliberately sought to turn the Jewish people away from the Father by calling us to look downward to Him, the Son? Are we supposed to believe that Yeshua would deliberately invite us Jews to look to Him if that "looking" caused us to forfeit an already correct relationship with God? That would make Jesus a deliberate deceiver of us Jews.

Yeshua is not just the Restorer of Israel, or just the Savior of the world. He's both.

Those who mistakenly advocate this argument need to be very careful. Whether they realize it or not, they're making serious accusations against the Lord.

JESUS: RESTORER OF ISRAEL, LIGHT OF THE WORLD

God declared through the prophet Isaiah, "It is too small a thing that You should be My Servant to raise up the tribes of Jacob and to restore the preserved ones of Israel; I will also make You a light of the nations so that My salvation may reach to the end of the earth" (Isa. 49:6). One of the pivotal words in that verse is a word that we may so easily overlook. It's the word *also*. Because of that word, we understand clearly that Yeshua is not just the Restorer of Israel, or just the Savior of the world. He's both. There are not two ways of salvation, nor are there two Saviors.

Jesus is the Light of the world, but the world certainly includes the Jews. Jesus is the Light of the nations, but that Light is not just from the Jews; that Light is for the Jews as well.

> "Arise, shine; for your light has come, and the glory of the LORD has risen upon you. For behold, darkness will cover the earth and deep darkness the peoples; but the LORD will rise upon you and His glory will appear upon you. Nations will come to your light, and kings to the brightness of your rising." (Isa. 60:1–3)

> "A light of revelation to the Gentiles, *and* the glory of Your people Israel." (Luke 2:32)

Jesus is the light of the Gentiles *because* He is the restorer of the Jews. If He's not the One who will raise up the tribes of Jacob, then neither is He the One who brings God's salvation to the ends of the earth.

CHAPTER 10

"The Church Needs to Repent, Not Proclaim"

I've been told . . .

> "Since there's so much anti-Semitism in the church, and since so much evil has been done to Jews in the name of Christ, Christians need to repent and ask Jews to forgive them before they can tell them about the Lord."

SO MANY CRIMES against the Jewish people can be traced to the anti-Jewish teachings of the church: charges of deicide by church fathers; legal writs against us during the Dark Ages; the slaughter of European Jewish communities by Crusaders on their way to "liberate" the Holy Land; the expulsions, tortures, executions, and forced baptisms of the Inquisition; the blood libels and pogroms in Europe and Russia. Moreover, anti-Semitic teaching in the church was a significant factor in the support and condoning of the Nazis shown by many in the church during the Holocaust. It's little wonder why we

Jews find it so hard to give Yeshua a fair and impartial hearing. The loving message of what He accomplished for all of us through the shedding of His blood at Calvary is obscured by the shedding of Jewish blood at the hands of those who claimed to love, follow, and belong to Him.

ONCE, IN ODESSA

I remember a conversation I had in Odessa, Ukraine, with an older Christian woman, back in the 1990s. She told me, "In light of all that's happened to your people in the name of Christ, I would never offend them by telling them about the Lord."

"What would you say instead?" I asked.

"As a Christian, I'd apologize to them."

"For . . . ?" I prompted.

"For *everything*," she said. "Especially for the Holocaust."

She was old enough to remember the Second World War, so I asked, "Did you support the Holocaust?"

"No," she protested, apparently shocked that I would even suggest such a thing.

"Did Yeshua support the Holocaust?"

Again, she answered with an emphatic "no."

"Then why would you apologize for something that neither you nor Jesus supported?"

She grimaced, clearly annoyed with my inability to grasp what was obvious to her. "Because your people think that Jesus is the cause of the Holocaust."

"Yes, some of us do," I admitted. "And your apology in His name and on His behalf lets us continue believing that lie."

Repentance for past sins and denunciation of present expressions of anti-Semitism are very much in order—when properly done. But apologies can be a tricky thing. We need to be very clear about what we want to communicate. For example, if I apologize to someone for a particular sin, then that person has the right to understand that I'm personally guilty of that sin, unless I make it clear that I'm apologizing on behalf of someone else. And if I do apologize for someone else—say, for my relative who's disgraced and dishonored the family name—then hopefully the person to whom I apologize will understand that my *relative* has committed that sin, not me.

In fact, I'd also hope that the one to whom I've apologized will understand two more important points: first, I'm disowning and condemning the actions of my relative, and second, I'm declaring that my relative's crimes should not be taken as characteristic of the family whose name has been dishonored. My relative's crimes don't describe my family. Rather, they describe my relative alone.

So while it is right to ask forgiveness for the crimes of the church, it is not right to apologize on Yeshua's behalf. Jesus has done no wrong. Yeshua is not guilty of the crimes that evil men and women committed in His name any more than modern medicine is guilty of the crimes that Dr. Mengele, the monster of Auschwitz, committed against the Jewish people in the name of medical science.

If a Christian apologizes for the anti-Semitic crimes of the church, it needs to be clear that those crimes were committed by sinful individuals whose actions were a complete contradiction of everything that Jesus taught.

The purpose of repentance is not to increase the believer's burden of guilt over generational sins. Rather, it's to free the believer from the penalty and the shackles of those sins.

And what if we're not guilty ourselves? Should we still apologize for sins committed by our families or by our nation? At times, yes. But that apology should follow genuine repentance before the *Lord*. Consider the example of Daniel (Dan. 9:4-6). Deeply grieved by the long history of rebellion and disobedience that ultimately led to our captivity in Babylon, Daniel identified with the people's sins and brought his burden of guilt before the Lord.

God is the One who forgives, even if and when people can't. We must repent before God and seek His forgiveness first.

And again, we need to be careful: The purpose of repentance is not to increase the believer's burden of guilt over generational sins. Rather, it's to free the believer from the penalty and the shackles of those sins. Wonderfully, the chain to a family's sins is broken by Yeshua's cross.

THE FRUIT OF REPENTANCE

There's a significant difference between remembering the sin, and continuing to carry the guilt and condemnation of that sin after genuine repentance has been made, and after forgiveness has been received from the Lord. Paul never forgot the crimes that he committed against the church. He admits, "I used to persecute the church of God beyond measure and tried to destroy it . . . I was formerly a blasphemer and a persecutor and a violent aggressor" (Gal. 1:13; 1 Tim. 1:13).

But the active memory of his sin didn't cause him to live his life burdened by guilt and trapped in an unending pursuit of forgiveness. Rather, the remembrance of his sin deepened his wonder over God's mercy and grace. "Yet I was shown mercy because I acted ignorantly in unbelief; and the grace of our Lord was more than abundant" (1 Tim. 1:13–14).

What should follow genuine repentance? What should be the discernable fruit? Not only a change of heart and conduct but also a declaration of God's grace.

When David confessed his sins of adultery and murder to the Lord, he received God's pardon. As a result, an overwhelming gratitude and love flooded his heart to such a degree that his lips burst forth with praise and proclamation.

> How blessed is he whose transgression is forgiven, whose sin is covered! . . . I said, "I will confess my transgressions to the LORD"; and You forgave the guilt of my sin . . . Many are the sorrows of the wicked, but he who trusts in the LORD, lovingkindness shall surround him. Be glad in the LORD and rejoice, you righteous ones; and shout for joy, all you who are upright in heart. (Ps. 32:1, 5, 10–11)

Three centuries later, the prophet Isaiah described the exuberant proclamation that ought to follow if our repentance is sincere.

> Then you will say on that day, "I will give thanks to You, O LORD; for although You were angry with me, Your anger is turned away, and You comfort me. Behold, God is my salvation, I will trust and not be

afraid; for the LORD GOD is my strength and song, and He has become my salvation" . . . And in that day you will say, "Give thanks to the LORD, call on His name. *Make known His deeds among the peoples; make them remember that His name is exalted."* Praise the LORD in song, for He has done excellent things; *let this be known throughout the earth. Cry aloud and shout for joy,* O inhabitant of Zion, for great in your midst is the Holy One of Israel." (Isa. 12:1–2, 4–6)

Saul of Tarsus, the persecutor of the early church, also followed his repentance with proclamation: "and immediately he began to proclaim Jesus in the synagogues, saying, 'He is the Son of God'" (Acts 9:20).

Receiving God's forgiveness must be followed by *proclaiming* God's forgiveness. We're commanded to make His deeds known. From repentance, to pardon, to proclamation for the sake of those who haven't yet believed. Isn't that the pattern that we see?

Something's not right when Christians repeatedly ask God and us Jews to forgive the sins of the church, but then fail to demonstrate one of the most important fruits of repentance: the fruit of joyous proclamation; the unashamed declaration that the blood of Yeshua cleanses us of all sin; the affirmation that His cleansing is available to all who confess.

If your heart is burdened because of the church's sinful past, and if you feel it's appropriate for you to repent, either for your own sins or for the transgressions of others, then by all means, repent. But make the repentance genuine, not unending and routine. Trust God's promise to cleanse you of all unrighteousness (1 John 1:9). Believe His assurance that the guilt and condemnation have been taken away (Rom. 8:1). Receive His complete pardon. Taste the joy that comes from receiving His forgiveness. And let your lips proclaim what God has done in your life, so that others may come to Him. That's what David did.

> Restore to me the joy of Your salvation and sustain me with a willing spirit. Then I will teach transgressors Your ways, and sinners will be converted to You. (Ps. 51:12–13)

CHAPTER 11

"Aliyah (Immigrating to Israel) Is the Real Priority"

I've been told . . .

> "It's more important to bring the Jewish people back to the land of Israel rather than tell them about the Lord. Making Aliyah—returning to Israel—is the first priority. Redemption will follow once all the Jews are back in the Land."

I BELIEVE VERY FIRMLY that a day is coming when God will regather all the Jewish people to the Land. But do the Scriptures teach that the physical *regathering* of Israel must precede the spiritual *redemption* of Israel?

To be sure, important passages such as Ezekiel 36:24–25 clearly teach that God will bring many of us back to Israel before He saves us: "For I will take you from the nations, gather you from all the lands and bring you into your own land. Then I will sprinkle clean water on you, and you will be clean; I will cleanse you from all your filthiness and from all your idols." But a number of other passages in the Hebrew Scriptures also declare that *first* we must repent in the lands of our exile, and *then* God will bring us back to the Land of Israel. In fact, the earliest passages in the Bible that speak of our return to the Land state very clearly that repentance precedes the return. For example:

> "So it shall be when all of these things have come upon you, the blessing and the curse which I have set before you, and you call them to mind *in all the nations where the* LORD *your God has banished you,* and you return to the LORD your God and obey Him with all your heart and soul according to all that I command you today, you and your sons, *then* the LORD your God will restore you from captivity, and have compassion on you, and will gather you again from all the peoples where the LORD your God has scattered you." (Deut. 30:1–3)

Ezekiel 20:34–38 tells us the very same thing.

> "I will bring you out from the peoples and gather you from the lands where you are scattered, with a mighty hand and an outstretched arm and with wrath poured out; and I will bring you into the wilderness of the peoples, and there I will enter into judgment with you face to face. As I entered into judgment with your fathers in the wilderness of the land of Egypt, so I will enter into judgment with you," declares the Lord GOD. "I will make you pass under the rod, and *I will bring you into the bond of the covenant*; and I will purge from you the rebels and those who transgress against Me; *I will bring*

them out of the land where they sojourn, but they will not enter the land of Israel."

According to this passage, God will bring us into "the bond of the covenant" promised to us in Jeremiah 31:31–34 while we're still en route to Israel. But those who refuse to enter into that covenant will not enter the Land. This shouldn't surprise us, because God is always consistent with Himself: just as the first generation that left Egypt was not permitted to enter the land because of unbelief, so a later generation will be barred from entry for the same reason—the sin of unbelief.

So, according to Deuteronomy 30 and Ezekiel 20, God first brings us to faith in the Diaspora and purges the rebels from our midst, *then* He brings us back into the Promised Land.

But how can this be in light of Ezekiel 36? It's not a case of "either/or," but of "both/and." Some Jewish people will not return to the Land until they've repented in the exile; others will repent only after returning to the Land.

But what's common—and even central—to both scenarios? It's the fact that God wants us to repent and come back to Him. All these passages make it clear that the primary issue on God's heart is not His people's relocation, but His people's redemption.

God will indeed bring us back to the Land. But foremost on God's heart is not when we're standing in the Land, but whether we're standing on the Rock.

If relocation is the key to the redemption, and if national Aliyah is the prerequisite for the Lord's return, then we should wonder why we find no calls to come back to the Land in any of the preaching throughout the book of Acts or in the epistles of the apostles. Peter and Paul ministered to Jews in the exile. And so did all the other apostles and disciples who were scattered abroad. Though Israel still existed under Roman occupation as a geopolitical state at that time, the number of Jewish people living in the Diaspora was extensive, with thriving Jewish communities throughout the Roman and Parthian empires. Significant Jewish populations were found in Rome and Alexandria, to name just two. But nowhere in the New Testament do we find the disciples exhorting us to return to the Land. Instead, we find them exhorting us to repent and receive the Lord.

God's promises concerning the Land are true, guaranteed, and eternal. And so are His promises concerning our return. However, the central issue is not the timing of our restoration to the Land, but the moment of our restoration to the Lord. God will indeed bring us back to the Land. But foremost on God's heart is not when we're standing in the Land, but whether we're standing on the Rock.

CHAPTER 12

"Reconciliation Must Come First"

I've been told . . .

> "There can be no effective proclamation to the Jewish people unless Jews and Christians are reconciled to each other first."

SOME YEARS AGO, a pastor invited me to speak at a conference dedicated to the theme "How to Pray for Israel."

When I arrived, the pastor told me about a person at the conference whom I'll call Piotr. "You really need to meet and talk with him," the pastor told me. When I asked him why, he explained that Piotr had a great love for my people, but that his love was weighted down by a heavy burden of guilt. Piotr's father had played a central role in one of the truly horrific episodes of the Holocaust, when several hundred Jewish men, women, and children were deliberately burned alive. "His father was one of the men who set the fire," the pastor told me.

"You're right," I admitted softly. "I need to meet and talk with this man."

The longing for reconciliation abides in the hearts of many Gentiles and Jews. And by God's grace, reconciliation between us *is* possible for anyone who desires it. But there's a catch: in order for Jews and Gentiles to experience genuine and thorough reconciliation with each other, each of us must first be reconciled to God through the Messiah Yeshua.

There can be no true reconciliation between us without the cross. There can be no true peace without the Prince of Peace. Why? Because *He* is our peace; because *He* makes us one; because only *He* can break down the walls of enmity that separate us.

Sadly, there are Christians who believe that the way to reconciliation with us Jews is by denying or keeping silent about what Yeshua accomplished on the cross. Because so much evil has been committed against the Jewish people by false Christians "in the name of Christ," some genuine Christians try to purchase the friendship of Jewish people by choosing to say nothing about Yeshua and His atoning work. They love the Jewish people, but they deliberately avoid saying anything about the One who has planted that love in their hearts. In essence, they want to be loved back by us more than they want us to experience the love of the Lord for ourselves. So, the greatest demonstration of God's love for us—the sacrificing of His Son for the

Biblical reconciliation speaks of a state of unity and harmony that exists only because it rests on a new foundation—a relationship of love.

payment of our sins (John 3:16; Rom. 5:8)—is deliberately omitted from any discussion for fear of alienating the Jewish person whose affections are so desperately sought.

This is tragic. By keeping silent about Jesus and His love for His Jewish people, Christians only reinforce the common thinking among some of us that Jesus really *was* responsible for the Crusades, the Inquisition, the pogroms, and the Holocaust. Silence about the gospel cannot purchase reconciliation with the Jewish people. Silence merely reinforces the lie that the gospel is a message against us Jews.

THE WAY OF BIBLICAL RECONCILIATION

The biblical notion of reconciliation or peace between former enemies means so much more than the mere absence of hostilities or the cessation of strife. Biblical reconciliation speaks of a state of unity and harmony that exists only because it rests on a new foundation—a relationship of love. But that love is not possible without a mutual change of heart. And that change of heart is not possible without the Messiah Yeshua's cleansing intervention in our lives. Once we understand how God in His grace has forgiven us for all the sins we've committed against Him, only then can we find the enabling grace to forgive those who have sinned against us.

Comprehending the way God has dealt with us is the key to our dealings with others. If we truly grasp how Yeshua has forgiven us, then we're provoked to forgive others. If we truly perceive the depth of Yeshua's mercy toward us, then we're compelled to be merciful to those who've injured us. Knowing how deeply Yeshua loves us, despite all the crimes we've committed against Him, empowers us to love the ones He's commanded us to love, no matter what injustices we've suffered at their hands.

Jews cannot love Gentiles rightly until the Messiah is loved first. And we cannot love Him first unless we hear and believe what He did for us out of His incomprehensible love.

It's easy to see the inadequacy of the type of "reconciliation" that the world offers people. A ruling from a court or a governmental law might rectify an injustice or resolve a dispute. But can a legal ruling reconcile the hearts of the parties in the dispute? Can it cause the injured party to love the one who caused the injury? Can it fill the heart of the victim with compassion for the perpetrator of the injustice? There is no loving embrace between opposing parties who have been "reconciled" to each other through legal writ or political decree.

I told him that because of the Messiah, we were now related. God had made us "family." And our relationship as brothers in the Lord was greater than his physical relationship with his father who was now dead.

We need to ask ourselves the uncomfortable question: "Can the mere acknowledgment of the evil of the Holocaust and other crimes against the Jewish people bring about reconciliation? Can condemnation of the crime by the criminals' children accomplish genuine reconciliation between Christians and Jews while the terrifying images of history cling so vividly to our minds?"

No, but what's impossible for us is not impossible for God. Reconciliation *is* possible, but only through the cross. Let me come back to my story about Piotr, the man whose father had murdered Jewish people during the Holocaust.

As I walked up to Piotr at the conference, his face grew noticeably tense, even fearful. I quickly sought to take that tension and fear away. "I know you're in a lot of pain over the past," I told him.

"Do you know why?"

"Yes," I said. "I know." We sat down beside each other, and I continued to tell him what was in my heart. I told him that because of the Messiah, we were now related. God had made us "family." And our relationship as brothers in the Lord was greater than his physical relationship with his father who was now dead. At the end of our talk, we prayed together. Two days later, I received some wonderful news from the pastor who had coordinated the conference. He told me that Piotr had written an email to tell him that the burden he'd carried for so many years because of his father's guilt had finally fallen away. What a privilege God had given me by letting me be an instrument to lift that weight.

Without Yeshua, Piotr and I might have become friends. But in the world, no matter how close the friendship, he would always have been to me, first and foremost, the son of the man who had murdered my people. But because of Yeshua, Piotr and I could be more than friends; he and I could be family.

FIRST ESTRANGED, THEN RECONCILED

The Bible explains that all of us—Jews and non-Jews—are initially cut off from God because of our sins. Speaking through

Isaiah, the Lord told Israel, "But your iniquities have made a separation between you and your God, and your sins have hidden His face from you so that He does not hear" (Isa. 59:2).

Centuries later, speaking through the apostle Paul, God told a non-Jewish assembly essentially the very same thing: "remember that you were at that time [before believing in Yeshua] separate from Christ, excluded from the commonwealth of Israel, and strangers to the covenants of promise, having no hope and without God in the world" (Eph. 2:12).

That's the bad news of estrangement. And now comes the good news of reconciliation:

> But God, being rich in mercy, because of His great love with which He loved us, even when we were dead in our transgressions, made us alive together with Christ (by grace you have been saved), and raised us up with Him, and seated us with Him in the heavenly places in Christ Jesus . . . now in Christ Jesus you who formerly were far off have been brought near by the blood of Christ. (Eph. 2:4–6, 13)

And because He has reconciled each of us to Himself, *now* we can be reconciled to each other. Now, and only now, can we be made one in Him, for

> He Himself is our peace, who made both groups into one and broke down the barrier of the dividing wall by abolishing in His flesh the enmity . . . that in Himself He might make the two into one new man, thus establishing peace, and might reconcile them both in one body to God through the cross. (Eph. 2:14–16)

MESSENGERS OF
BIBLICAL RECONCILIATION

And since we have been reconciled to each other through Yeshua's work on the cross and through our cleaving to the message of the gospel, what does God want us to do? Again God tells us through the words of Paul. "God . . . reconciled us to Himself through Christ and gave us the ministry of reconciliation" (2 Cor. 5:18).

Now that we're reconciled to each other through Him, He explains that He's placed that ministry of reconciliation into our hands. That means we must take it to others. And what is that ministry of reconciliation? It's the ministry of the proclamation of a message. "God was in Christ reconciling the world to Himself . . . Therefore, we are ambassadors for Christ . . . we beg you on behalf of Christ, be reconciled to God" (2 Cor. 5:19–20).

According to the Bible, the ministry of reconciliation is the proclamation of reconciliation through the cross. In other words, the ministry of reconciliation starts with the declaration of the good news.

Some people look forward to a day when more Jews, Germans, Poles, Russians, Hungarians, Arabs, and everyone else will be able to shake hands in cordial accord. I labor for the day when more and more Jews, Germans, Poles, Russians, Hungarians, Arabs—and everyone else—will throw their arms around each other's necks and greet each other with a holy kiss.

That reconciliation is possible—but not without the message of the cross.

CHAPTER 13

"Silent Love Speaks Louder than Gospel Words"

I've been told . . .

> "Silent love is a much more powerful and persuasive testimony at this time than speaking openly and directly to Jewish people about the Lord."

IN THE EARLY 1990s, a newly reunited Germany opened her doors to Jewish immigration from the former USSR. Germany adopted this policy for at least two reasons: to make amends for the Holocaust, and to change her image from being a country that hated Jews to a country that harbored Jews against a hostile world. As a result, the unforeseeable occurred. Tens of thousands of Russian-speaking Jewish immigrants began a westward trek to Germany—to a land where most of us Jews thought we would never return. At the start of the immigration, the Jewish population in Germany stood at approximately 31,000. By 2005, the number of immigrants had swollen to over 230,000. In a span of just twelve to fifteen years, Germany had become the third largest Jewish population center in Western Europe, surpassed only by France and the United Kingdom. The return of all these Jewish people to German cities posed an extremely uncomfortable question to German believers in Jesus: What, if anything, should they say to their new Jewish neighbors about the Lord?

ONCE, IN THE RUHR VALLEY

I took my first trip to Germany in the spring of 1995. I was living in Moscow at the time, but I wanted to see firsthand the Jewish immigration to Germany, and I wanted to know how German pastors felt about it. One evening, after speaking in a church in the Ruhrgebiet (Ruhr Valley), the pastor and I sat in the emptied sanctuary and talked late into the night. We'd never met before. But a common love for our Lord and a common concern for the Jewish refugees built a bridge that enabled us to speak heart to heart, as though we'd been friends for years. At one point, the pastor (whom I'll call Hartmut) said to me, "Avi, I know that God is bringing these Jewish people back to Germany as a way of giving us a second chance. But I just don't believe that we Germans can tell your people about Jesus."

Though I could second-guess what his answer would be, I asked him, "Why not?"

"Because of the Holocaust," he answered, predictably. "I feel we Germans have forfeited the right to talk with Jews about the Lord."

Gently, I disagreed. "You not only have the right," I offered.

"You have the responsibility." I went on to tell him how I believed that God was bringing the Jewish people back to Germany for at least three reasons: because of His love for the Jewish people, because of His love for the German church, and because of His love for the German people. "God wants my people to hear the gospel and be saved. He wants German believers to know the joy of being used by God to bring His people to Himself. He wants *Germans* to hear the gospel from Jewish lips. And I think He wants the world to see Jews and Germans proclaiming the gospel together. What a testimony of the love of the Lord. What a testimony of the reconciling power of the cross."

At first, Hartmut nodded enthusiastically, and I could tell that my vision for the future had touched his heart. But then the nodding came to an abrupt halt. Apparently, a darker vision from the past had intruded upon his mind. After a moment, he said, "We can't, Avi. We can't talk with your people about Jesus."

"So what do you think German Christians should do instead?" I asked.

Hartmut spoke slowly, as though he were walking through the mental landscape as he took each step. "We should love the Jewish people. We should help them whenever we can. But as far as Jesus is concerned, I think we should be silent."

"Silent," I repeated.

"Yes," he said, quietly but emphatically. "About Jesus, we should be silent."

I changed the subject, and we talked of other things. He told me a little bit about his family, and I told him a little bit about mine. He told me about some previous churches in which he'd served as pastor, and I told him how challenging it had been for my wife and me to move from the convenience of the States to the chaos of the Soviet Union back in 1991. Then I brought the conversation back to the tender topic we'd been discussing a few minutes before.

"Hartmut, there were genuine Christians in Germany during the war, weren't there?"

"Yes, of course," he said. He was old enough to remember going to church as a child during those times.

"You were silent. And now, fifty years after the war, God is bringing all these Jewish people back to Germany. And you're suggesting . . . silence."

"So what was the mistake, or the crime, or even the sin of the believing church back then?" I asked.

He answered automatically, without needing any time to think. "We were silent." Almost instantly, his face seemed to freeze, as though he were startled by the echo of his words.

"You were silent," I repeated softly. "And now, fifty years after the war, God is bringing all these Jewish people back to Germany. And you're suggesting . . . silence."

Not long after my meeting with Hartmut, a Russian-speaking Jewish refugee happened to wander into his church. For unknown reasons, the refugee was especially drawn by the prominence that was given to the name "Jesus" on the church marquee. Hartmut was there when Alex walked in, and when Alex asked about Jesus, Hartmut explained. He took his time, because it was clear from Alex's accent that

Hartmut was speaking to a newly arrived Russian-speaking Jewish immigrant. Despite the language barriers, Hartmut found the right words to explain the good news, and Alex listened. Hartmut ended the conversation by inviting Alex to their next church service, and the following Sunday, Alex and his wife, Inna, showed up.

They didn't understand a great deal at that first service, but they understood enough. More conversations with Hartmut took place over the next few weeks, and after a month, Alex and Inna gave their hearts to the Lord.

LOVE CARES ABOUT THE BELOVED

My wife and I have had three children, and we love them very much. Suppose they were dying of a lethal addiction; a cure existed, if administered, but if left untreated, the addiction always killed. Suppose this addiction was not only ravaging their bodies, but it had also warped their sense of reality— so much so that they couldn't grasp the fact that they were killing themselves. And let's say I faced a great likelihood of being reviled and rejected by my children if I told them that they were desperately ill and needed to take the cure. Let's say that even if I spoke to them in the most loving terms and under the most favorable conditions, they were very likely to reject my message and spurn me, the messenger, because they were deceived into thinking that they were fine.

What should I do? Should I muster the courage to tell them the truth with all the love I possessed but in terms clear enough for them to understand? Should I at least try to speak an initial word and lay the foundation for future talks? Or

All too often, our silence takes two tragic forms. We choose silence before people, and so we fail to speak. Or we choose silence before God, and we fail to pray.

should I keep silent out of a fear of their rejection? Should I risk letting them die, and tell myself that I did this out of love?

The Scripture exhorts us to speak the truth in love (Eph. 4:15). To speak the truth without love is often callous and counterproductive. But to speak in love while omitting the truth is inadequate and deceptive. If the omission is a matter of life and death, then the omission isn't just deceptive—it's deadly.

True love cannot be silent, if silence allows the beloved to die. True love cares more about the outcome facing the beloved than about the consequences facing the one who speaks. True love compels us to speak.

YESHUA'S LOVE

Jesus did not love us with a silent love. Yes, He fed our hungry with the loaves and the fish. Yes, He healed our lame, our blind, and our sick. Yes, He even raised our sons and daughters from the dead. But He also told us the truth. He told us the gospel, and He warned us that "unless you repent, you will all likewise perish" (Luke 13:3). When He spoke the truth in love and in no uncertain terms, He knew how we would react. He knew that many would repent and receive Him, and He knew that many others would revile and reject Him. But He had to tell us the truth. Love *compelled* Him to speak. Love *forbade* Him from keeping the truth to Himself.

Silence about the gospel is not love. Silence is the enemy

of the salvation of my people. Silence is the enemy of the salvation of any people. All too often, our silence takes two tragic forms. We choose silence before people, and so we fail to speak. Or we choose silence before God, and we fail to pray.

The prophet Isaiah loved his people and longed for their salvation. And so he cried,

> For Zion's sake I will not keep silent, and for Jerusalem's sake I will not keep quiet, until her righteousness goes forth like brightness, and her salvation like a torch that is burning. (Isa. 62:1)

CHAPTER 14

"It's Time to Comfort, Not Confront"

I've been told . . .

> "Telling Jewish people about Jesus isn't effective during times like ours. The world is growing more and more hostile to the Jews. Words of comfort and acts of solidarity are a much stronger testimony to Jewish people than telling them about the Lord."

IN ISAIAH 40, we see so clearly the heart of compassion that God possesses for His people. "'Comfort, O comfort My people,' says your God" (v. 1). But if we're commanded to comfort His people, then we need to ask ourselves the question, "How?" What form is that comfort supposed to take?

In the verse from Isaiah 40 mentioned above, the commandment to comfort is immediately followed by the commandment to speak a message. "Speak kindly to Jerusalem; and call out to her." In fact, the message *is* the comfort. But what's the message? At that time in Israel's history, the prophet was looking ahead to the time when Judah would have already endured God's judgment at the hands of the Babylonians, and so the comfort consisted of the message "that her warfare has ended, that her iniquity has been removed, that she has received of the LORD's hand double for all her sins" (Isa. 40:2).

Is there any greater message of comfort than the declaration from God Himself that peace is at hand and that the penalty for sin has been paid? That's the message that God pronounced in Isaiah 40:1–2, and that message hasn't changed over the centuries.

It's the message that our warfare is ended and we can have peace with God.

It's the pronouncement that our iniquity is removed by the atoning sacrifice of the Lord.

It's the good news that Yeshua died for our sins, that He was buried, and that He was raised from the dead on the third day, so that our iniquity may be removed and so that we may then have peace with God.

To comfort Israel is correct. But to comfort her without the message is not the model of comfort that the Lord gives us in this text.

SOMETIMES ACTIONS
DON'T SPEAK LOUDER THAN WORDS

Standing with Israel, speaking out against anti-Semitism, showing kindness to the Jewish people through acts of help and love—these are unquestionably the right things to do.

All of these actions may be a testimony that God will use to pry open closed hearts and draw people closer to Himself. But if Christians allow themselves to think that this much of a testimony is enough with no need for more, or if they allow themselves to believe that the Jewish people will understand the gospel message from these loving actions alone, then they are mistaken.

Acts of love and kindness are correct and biblical, and they are certainly part of a person's testimony. But acts of love and kindness alone don't communicate the content of the gospel. Rather, they *confirm* the content of the gospel, or they provoke a person to find out what the gospel is all about. Acts of love and kindness can attract people to the message, and they can substantiate that the message is true. But the content of the message must be heard, understood, and embraced.

Acts of love and kindness alone don't communicate the content of the gospel. Rather, they *confirm* the content of the gospel.

If it were sufficient simply to live a life that demonstrated the love of God without explaining the content of the gospel, then Yeshua Himself certainly would have won our hearts just by the way He lived. Who has lived a more godly life than God Himself when He walked among us on earth? And yet even He proclaimed the content of the gospel message. So if the perfect life of Yeshua alone wasn't a sufficient testimony back then, how can we think that our far-less-than-perfect lives are sufficient testimonies today?

All of us carry the responsibility of presenting a twofold testimony to the nonbelievers whom we know. We must proclaim

We must proclaim the content of the gospel message through the declaration of our lips, and we must demonstrate the truthfulness of that message through the caliber of our lives and through the depth of our love for others.

the content of the gospel message through the declaration of our lips, and we must demonstrate the truthfulness of that message through the caliber of our lives and through the depth of our love for others. God uses us in different ways in others' lives. But one way or another, the person who comes to faith is the person who has heard the message of God's redeeming love, who has tasted that love through the kindness of God's children, and who has responded to God's love with repentance and saving faith.

Too often, the comfort we offer is only the comfort that's comfortable for us to give. But that might not be the comfort that the person in distress needs to receive. Our comfort is empty or incomplete if we withhold what the person is due (Prov. 3:27–28). Or even worse, our comfort is false if we let people think that everything's fine when it's not. May God never have reason to say of us, "They have healed the brokenness of My people superficially" (Jer. 6:14).

THE COMFORT WE RECEIVED

In 2 Corinthians 1, Paul speaks of the responsibility to comfort others with "the comfort with which we ourselves are comforted by God" (v. 4). That certainly includes everything from words of empathy to acts of compassion. But is that all?

What's the greatest comfort that we who know the Lord have received? What's the greatest comfort that we can give?

It is the message that our warfare with God can end; that peace with God is available; that our iniquity can be removed because of the price that Yeshua paid for us at the cross.

By all means, comfort God's people in the midst of our mounting distress. Show your love by standing with Israel and by performing acts of compassion. Cry out against anti-Semitism. But don't rest until you have reason to believe that your Jewish friend has heard the content of the message that God has commanded us to proclaim: Yeshua's death and resurrection put an end to the war between humanity and God. Iniquity has been removed for those who place their trust in Him. It may not be a comfortable comfort to extend, but it's the comfort that my people need to receive.

CHAPTER 15

"Jewish Evangelism Is Finishing the Work That Hitler Started"

I've been told . . .

> "Jewish evangelism is anti-Semitic. By proclaiming the gospel to the Jewish people, you're finishing the work that Hitler began. It's nothing less than spiritual genocide, the spiritual destruction of the Jewish people, and a continuation of the Shoah under a different name and by different means."

HOW COULD THAT POSSIBLY be the case? Jesus and the apostles preached the gospel to us Jews. In fact, Moses and all the prophets preached the gospel to us Jews (e.g., Isaiah 53). Does that mean that Moses, the prophets, the apostles, and Jesus were like spiritual Nazis seeking to destroy the Jewish people with a spiritual holocaust? Clearly that would be an absurd conclusion.

In love and compassion, Yeshua told a Jewish audience, "Unless you believe that I am He, you will die in your sins" (John 8:24). In the same vein, He told the apostles, all of whom were Jews, "no one comes to the Father but through Me" (John 14:6). The apostle Peter told the Sanhedrin, the Jewish high court, "there is no other name [besides Jesus] under heaven that has been given among men by which we must be saved" (Acts 4:12). And the apostle Paul said that the gospel message is the power of God unto salvation "to the Jew first" (Rom. 1:16). In light of the biblical record, we need to ask ourselves an extremely uncomfortable but crucial question: *If the above claims are true, and if we Jews will indeed die in our sins unless we believe in Jesus, then who is guilty of committing the anti-Jewish act? The one who communicates the gospel message, or the one who withholds that message of salvation?*

INADVERTENT ANTI-SEMITISM

By God's grace, there are undoubtedly multitudes of Christians worldwide whose hearts are filled with a deep and fervent love for the Jewish people. And yet, paradoxically and tragically, some of them denounce the very ministry that Jesus Himself ardently pursued and prioritized throughout His three-year ministry on earth—bringing the good news to the lost sheep of Israel. Most likely, these Christians believe that by disavowing the cause of Jewish evangelism, they're expressing friendship and respect for the unbelieving Jewish people whom they love. But by denouncing Jewish evangelism, these Christians aren't extending an act of friendship or love. Rather, they're committing the most unloving and anti-Jewish act that a Christian can commit. They're advocating that Jews be denied the only information that can rescue us from spiritual destruction, and they're advocating this only and specifically because we're Jews!

I'm not saying that Christians who oppose Jewish evangelism are necessarily anti-Semites. But if no one comes to the Father except through the Son, then how can a denunciation of Jewish evangelism be anything other than an anti-Jewish act? It is anti-Semitic because it contributes to the spiritual destruction of the Jewish people. This contribution to our spiritual destruction is the real continuation of the Shoah.

Someone might argue, "But we didn't know!" But can anyone honestly claim ignorance when the Scriptures are so clear? And what about when the veil is lifted? What if a Christian sees clearly from the Scripture that without Jesus, we Jews face eternal destruction just like everyone else? And yet, what if that Christian continues to stand by in silence, or worse, continues to denounce the communication of God's message of rescue to the Jewish people?

If a doctor withheld lifesaving treatment from a group of patients specifically because they were Jewish, would that doctor be heralded as a friend of the Jews?

I can understand the motives of nonbelievers who call Jewish evangelism a continuation of the Holocaust. They think they're shielding my people from a message that they mistakenly assume to be hateful or harmful to us Jews. I can even understand the motives of other nonbelievers who realize that the accusation is false, but who use the accusation all the same. They know that the emotional force of the accusation accomplishes two anti-missionary goals: it frightens Christians away from sharing the gospel, and it frightens Jewish people away from listening to what Christians have to say.

But what about sincere fellow believers in Jesus who know better? What about genuine Christians who understand what the Bible says, but who echo the argument that Jewish evangelism is anti-Semitic, or who promote the argument by keeping silent? What about believers who allow the Jewish people to think that God's message of love for them is a message of hate?

What can motivate a genuine believer in Jesus to commit such an unconscionable mistake? One of the greatest reasons is the fear of rejection from the people whom the Christian loves, and I'll talk more about that later. But there's another very powerful reason, and it has to do with our struggle between what we *prefer* to be true, and what we *know* to be true.

EXALTING PREFERENCE OVER SCRIPTURE

Sometimes our beliefs spring from personal preferences. We listen first to our hearts instead of studying the Scriptures. In this way, we're very much like atheists who refuse to consider whether God might exist. The problem isn't a lack of evidence or an ambiguity about what the Scriptures say. The problem is a pre-commitment in our hearts, based on what we want to be true.

Too often, in our hearts, we *want* Jewish evangelism to be unnecessary. The consoling thought that Jews don't need the gospel takes the Jewish people spiritually out of harm's way. It eases our consciences over our failure to pray for Israel's salvation, and it pacifies our hearts when we're troubled over our reluctance to take an open stand in favor of an unpopular cause. It also softens our guilt over our refusal to share the gospel when God gives us opportunities to speak. We *want* Jewish evangelism to be unnecessary. So we fashion our theology to suit our desires, and then we justify and substantiate our position with Scripture taken out of context, rather than basing our theology first on what the Scripture has to say.

Let me sound an earnest alarm.

Voices in the church have followed this tendency of building a theology on a pre-commitment to preference at least twice in recent decades, contributing to the physical and spiritual harm of the Jewish people. Eight decades ago, men and women claiming to be Christians actively supported or silently condoned the anti-Semitic policies of Fascism. Then, after the fact, these voices justified the stance theologically through a selective misuse and misappropriation of Scripture. "Doesn't the Old Testament prophet Isaiah call the Jews a 'sinful nation, people weighed down with iniquity, offspring of evil doers' (Isa. 1:4)?" these voices argued. "And doesn't the New Testament say, 'You are of your father the devil' (John 8:44)?" So misapplied Scriptures were used to support a pre-commitment of the heart.

Now segments within the church are condemning Jewish evangelism. And just as before, the present position is theologically justified after the fact by a selective misuse of Scripture. "Doesn't the Old Testament call the Jews 'chosen?' And doesn't Paul say that 'all Israel will be saved?'"

Eighty years ago, that tendency of following the heart, then constructing the theology led to the abandonment, betrayal, and destruction of one-third of my people. Today, that same tendency is placing the Jewish people's spiritual well-being in the gravest peril. Ironically, the first instance occurred as a result of undisguised hate, but today it's occurring in the name of love.

If we condemn Jewish evangelism as anti-Semitic, how close do we come to condemning the greatest Jewish evangelist of all time, the Messiah Jesus Himself? If we brand Jewish evangelism as a spiritual continuation of the Holocaust, how close do we come to branding Jesus as a destroyer of the people whom He loves and longs to save?

I know that my words must sting, especially for those whose hearts are already grieved by the church's collusion with the Nazi regime, either through silence or active support. But it's better to hear these words from me, a brother in the Lord, and a Jew. "Faithful are the wounds of a friend" (Prov. 27:6).

CHAPTER 16

"Jewish Evangelism Is an Attack on Judaism"

I've been told . . .

> "Jewish evangelism seeks to convert the Jews, and therefore, it is an attack on the integrity of the Jewish faith. It's an intolerant, unloving, and arrogant affront. Even worse, it's an act of aggression, an attack on the continued existence of the Jews."

WHY IS IT INTOLERANT if we speak the truth? Why is it unloving if we speak that truth in love? Why is it arrogant if we implore a person to embrace the same life-saving truth that rescued our own lives from imminent danger? And why is it an act of aggression if we tell Jewish people that the Hope of Israel has come?

THE DARK HISTORY OF "CONVERSION"

I understand very well the knee-jerk reaction of hostility toward efforts to "convert" the Jewish people. Images of forced baptisms, confessions under torture, ultimatums to "convert" or die, and instances of slaying the "converted" anyway, just to be safe, all come to our minds from a history that's plagued by "Christian" attacks on Jewish life. I'm not advocating that the church resurrect the godless, monstrous practices that were used in the past to "convert" the Jewish people.

Biblical conversion according to the Jewish prophets is a matter of "turning around"—a change of mind, heart, and direction. Over and over again, we're called to turn away from our own self-destructive ways by turning back to God.

> "Therefore say to the house of Israel, 'Thus says the-Lord GOD, "Repent and turn away from your idols and turn your faces away from all your abominations."'" (Ezek. 14:6)

> "Repent and turn away from all your transgressions, so that iniquity may not become a stumbling block to you." (Ezek. 18:30)

> "Turn back, turn back from your evil ways! Why then will you die, O house of Israel?" (Ezek. 33:11)

Biblical conversion aims at spiritual restoration. By contrast, the despicable actions committed against us in the past illustrate the fact that in reality, the church's goal was not the biblical conversion of the Jewish people, but containment and subjugation.

Conversion is a matter of the heart, and people are "converted" when they respond to God's love, receive God's forgiveness, and turn back to God by forsaking their unbelief. A change of heart is precipitated by an appeal to the heart, not by a contest between beliefs. By all means, the church must forsake the ungodly mindset and methods that were used to "convert" the Jews. But the church must not forsake her God-given mandate to bring God's message of redeeming love to anyone, including the Jews.

JUDAISM UNDER ATTACK?

Jewish evangelism is not an attack on the integrity of modern-day Judaism. But it does challenge the supposed *adequacy* of Judaism when it comes to the question of how we can be saved. The gospel message challenges the notion that contemporary Judaism in any of its present forms can secure God's pardon and deliver us from the power of sin in our daily lives. Of course, the gospel doesn't just challenge contemporary Judaism in that way. The gospel challenges the notion that *any* religion, philosophy, or way of life can provide a solution to the problem of our sin. The Bible takes the exclusive position that only the gospel message is the power of God unto salvation, "to the Jew first and also to the Greek" (Rom. 1:16).

To be honest, this challenge is nothing new. God spoke very clearly against the vain hope that Gentiles placed in their false gods. For example, in Isaiah 45:16, He declared, "They will be put to shame and even humiliated, all of them; the manufacturers of idols will go away together in humiliation."

When it came to castigating us Jews for trusting in our own rituals and teachings, God was no less severe:

> "This people draw near with their words and honor Me with their lip service, but they remove their hearts far from Me, and their reverence for Me consists of tradition learned by rote." (Isa. 29:13; see also Matt. 15:8–9)

God even seemed to speak unsparingly against the very ordinances that He Himself gave to us through Moses, when we practiced them with hypocritical hearts. In Isaiah, He declared,

> "What are your multiplied sacrifices to Me? . . . I have had enough of burnt offerings of rams and the fat of fed cattle . . . New moon and sabbath, the calling of assemblies—I cannot endure iniquity and the solemn assembly. I hate your new moon festivals and your appointed feasts." (Isa. 1:11, 13–14)

These words were not an attack on the integrity of biblical Judaism but rather an indictment of the Israelites' hypocrisy and faith in the supposed sufficiency of external religious observance.

In the same way, Paul spoke not against the Law that he loved but against the mindset that the Law was adequate to save. "We are Jews by nature," Paul wrote, "not sinners from among the Gentiles; nevertheless knowing that a man is not justified by the works of the Law but through faith in Christ Jesus" (Gal. 2:15–16).

Paul the fervent Jew (see Acts 22:1–3) upheld the integrity

of the Law by upholding the purpose of the Law—to lead us to the Lord so that we may be justified by faith. But he challenged the notion that the Law could accomplish something that it was never intended to do. He challenged the notion that biblical Judaism was adequate to save.

If *biblical* Judaism, with its heart intact, was not adequate to save, how can modern-day Judaism, with its heart removed, accomplish what biblical Judaism could not?

The heart of biblical Judaism consisted of an active priesthood that performed the Levitical sacrifices in the temple at Jerusalem. Today, no priesthood, no sacrifices, and no temple exist. The heart of Judaism has been removed. So then, if *biblical* Judaism, with its heart intact, was not adequate to save, how can modern-day Judaism, with its heart removed, accomplish what biblical Judaism could not? To say lovingly but plainly that it can't save is not an attack on the integrity of modern-day Judaism. It is a challenge to the notion that modern-day Judaism is adequate to make us right with God.

A bit earlier I spoke of my friend Steve Cohen who implored his former boyhood friend to believe in Yeshua *before* the Lord's return. I remember another time when Steve and I sat in the office of a Jewish businessman who'd invited us to speak with him over lunch. Early in the conversation, he asked Steve a point-blank question: "What went wrong in your life that made you look to Jesus? I want to know what you went looking for, what you think you couldn't have found in Judaism."

I remember Steve's gracious but honest reply. "What I

couldn't find," Steve said, "was a living relationship with the God of Abraham, Isaac, and Jacob."

This wasn't an attack on the integrity of contemporary Judaism. It was a challenge to modern-day Judaism's supposed adequacy to save us from our sin and restore us to our God.

Judaism cannot provide us with an intimate, everlasting relationship with the God of Israel. Neither can any other ritual or system of belief. Salvation can only be found in an individual, and that individual is Jesus. "I, even I, am the LORD, and there is no savior besides Me" (Isa. 43:11).

JEWS UNDER ATTACK?

But isn't Jewish evangelism an attack on the preservation of the Jewish people? Won't Jewish evangelism lead to assimilation and the disappearance of us Jews? If there's anything that our history should teach us, it is the wonderful and irrefutable fact that we Jews will always exist as a distinct people. That unalterable existence isn't because of any moral superiority, cultural resilience, or intellectual prowess on our part, as some might argue. It's based on God's boundless love for His chosen people, and on His faithfulness to His own word.

> Thus says the LORD, "If the heavens above can be measured and the foundations of the earth searched out below, then I will also cast off all the offspring of Israel for all that they have done," declares the LORD. (Jer. 31:37)

There's another reason that accounts for why God will always preserve our people, and that's because of the presence of a faithful remnant. There's a Jewish tradition about the *lamedvavnik,* the thirty-six righteous ones of any given generation, for whose sake the world is not destroyed. Though it's just a tradition, it hints at a biblical truth.

God preserves the nation, partly for the sake of the remnant. Again, He tells us through Isaiah, "Unless the LORD of hosts had left us a few survivors, we would be like Sodom, we would be like Gomorrah" (Isa. 1:9).

Faith in Yeshua is not a threat to Jewish existence but an affirmation of our identity as Jews. The God who saved us through our faith in Jesus is the God who deepens our Jewish identity through that same faith.

Faith in Yeshua is not a threat to Jewish existence but an affirmation of our identity as Jews. The God who saved us through our faith in Jesus is the God who deepens our Jewish identity through that same faith. More often than not, Jewish people who believe in Yeshua experience a heightened commitment to their Jewish heritage and roots. By coming to Jesus, we discover that we've come home.

Though the titles change from time to time, Messianic Judaism is nothing new. If we're familiar with the New Testament, then we know, of course, that all of the first followers of Jesus were Jews, and they never stopped regarding themselves as Jews. Decades after coming to faith, the apostle Paul declared to his countrymen in Jerusalem, "I am a Jew, born in Tarsus of Cilicia, but brought up in this city" (Acts 22:3). Perhaps less well known is the fact that there have always been Jewish believers who continue to identify wholeheartedly as Jews, and who pass that sense of self-identification on to their children and to their children's children as well. The growth of messianic congregations throughout the world today is a testimony to the reality that our faith in Yeshua has not diminished our identity as Jews. It has strengthened it.

And how could it be otherwise? After all, Jesus is the Jewish Messiah, promised to us throughout the Hebrew Scriptures. In the final analysis, it all comes down this: if Jesus really is the Jewish Messiah, then the most Jewish thing that we Jews can do is believe in Him.

There is another reason why we can say with certainty that faith in Jesus will not lead to the disappearance of the Jewish people: the irrevocable call on our lives to be a gospel witness to the rest of the world. God created us Jews to proclaim the excellence of the One who has called us out of darkness and into His marvelous light. He called us to be an evangelistic light to the nations. This is the only call that Israel, as a people, has ever received. And this is the call, according to the apostle Paul, that has not been revoked, "for the gifts and the calling of God are irrevocable" (Rom. 11:29). God has preserved us as a distinct people so that we may fulfill our unique calling. The day will come when we Jews proclaim the gospel worldwide, as Jews.

But the fulfillment of that call requires our faith in Jesus. Our faith in Jesus guarantees the coming of the day when Jewish missionaries will proclaim the good news throughout the world.

CHAPTER 17

"The Holocaust Has Made Jewish Evangelism All But Impossible"

I've been told . . .

> "The monstrosity of the Holocaust has made it virtually impossible for Christians to share their faith with Jewish people, and it has made it impossible for Jewish people to believe. Given those two tragic facts, God will neither hold Jewish people accountable for failing to believe in Yeshua, nor will He hold Christians accountable for refusing to share their faith with their Jewish friends, acquaintances, and relatives."

THERE'S A CHERISHED Passover tradition in which the youngest child at the *seder,* the Passover meal, asks four questions that the rest are obligated to answer. Let me borrow that tradition by raising four questions that we might prefer to leave unasked:

1) Has the Holocaust made it impossible for the Jewish people to hear the gospel and believe?

God has made it clear in Scripture that there is no salvation in any name other than in the name of the Lord. So if the Holocaust has rendered the Jewish people incapable of hearing the gospel and trusting in the only name that saves, then the anti-Semites have won. They've succeeded in guaranteeing the spiritual destruction of Israel by making it impossible for us to call on His name. They've proven that Gentile sin is greater than God's sovereign will, and they've proven that anti-Semitism can thwart God's ability to save.

These are horrific thoughts.

But God's plans cannot be thwarted, and He remains mighty to save. Scripture makes that clear enough. "For the LORD of hosts has planned, and who can frustrate it? And as for His stretched-out hand, who can turn it back?" (Isa. 14:27).

What the Scripture attests, history affirms—even the history of the Holocaust. I wish I could invite you to ask Manfred and Laura Wertheim, Rachmiel Frydland, Vera Schlamm, Eleazer Erbach, Rose Price, or Carl Flesch whether or not the Holocaust made it impossible for Jewish people to come to faith. These are just some of the many Jewish people who went through the inferno of the Holocaust but came to faith in Yeshua.

And what about the thousands upon thousands of Jewish people who have come to faith in the decades since the Holocaust? What about the Jewish people who are coming to faith all over the world today?

Despite the horrors of the Holocaust, Jewish men, women, and children are giving their hearts to the Jewish Messiah Jesus. To say that the Holocaust has made it impossible for us Jews to receive the gospel and be saved is to deny reality. The post-Holocaust fact of the matter is this: Jewish people are coming to faith every day.

2) Does the Holocaust absolve Jewish people from believing in Yeshua?

The stories of Holocaust survivors who later came to faith stand as a remarkable and thrilling testimony to the faithfulness of God. But those stories also stand as a sober indictment against any of us who would use the horror of the Holocaust as an excuse for refusing to consider Yeshua's claims. No one will be able to stand before the Lord and say, "The Holocaust made it impossible for us Jews in general, and for me in particular, to consider the gospel." Why? Because so many others did consider the gospel and believe, despite everything that they endured.

No matter how deeply the Holocaust may have seared our hearts, we know that we cannot blame Jesus for the actions of evil men and women who acted in complete contradiction of everything that Jesus taught. We cannot blame Jesus for the Holocaust any more than we can blame the science of engineering for the construction of the gas chambers.

But I don't want to minimize the difficulty of the matter.

As a result of the Holocaust, it's extremely difficult for many of us Jews to consider the gospel claims objectively. One of the greatest barriers that the Holocaust has erected is this: it has reinforced our difficulty in recognizing our own sin. The heart of the gospel message is the call to repent and receive the forgiveness of the God whom we've wronged. But as a result of the Holocaust, so many of us Jews view ourselves not as "sinners," but as "innocent victims."

That we Jews have been victims throughout history is undeniably true. And to this day we are still victimized in the press, in the political arena, in parts of the church, and by terrorists who want to drive us into the sea.

The Holocaust might make sharing faith with the Jewish people more difficult, though not impossible. But where greater difficulty exists, greater grace abounds.

But are we innocent victims? Yes and no. We're certainly innocent of the crimes and false accusations that anti-Semites have hurled at us throughout the centuries, from being uniquely responsible for the death of the Messiah, to poisoning wells and using "Christian" blood to make Passover matzahs, to promoting an international conspiracy aimed at taking over the world. But though we're innocent of these false accusations, we're still separated from God because of our own sin. Why? Because everyone is guilty of sin. Even the most pious of us. "Indeed, there is not a righteous man on earth who continually does good and who never sins" (Eccl. 7:20).

Because of the Holocaust, it is extremely difficult for us Jews to understand that, like everyone else, we're guilty before

God and we need to repent. The Holocaust presents a formidable barrier. But it's not an impenetrable barrier, thanks to the loving testimony of Christians who pray and speak, the power of God's word that pierces and divides, and the Holy Spirit who convicts our hearts and enables us to believe.

3) Has the Holocaust made it impossible for Christians to share their faith with Jewish people?

The Holocaust might make sharing faith with the Jewish people more difficult, though not impossible. But where greater difficulty exists, greater grace abounds. More often than not, God has used *Gentiles* as the primary "agents" in bringing Jewish people to faith, even in countries like Germany, Poland, and the former USSR. God often uses Messianic Jews and non-Jewish Christians in different but complementary ways to guide a Jewish person to faith in the Lord. But the indisputable fact is that God consistently uses sincere, compassionate Christians not only to demonstrate the love of the Lord, but to communicate the content of the gospel message and to introduce Jewish people to their Messiah.

God often uses Messianic Jews and non-Jewish Christians in different but complementary ways to guide a Jewish person to faith in the Lord.

How can that be, in light of all that has happened? Grace. You and I may think it's simply impossible for Gentiles to be an effective gospel witness to the Jewish people. But as we know, what's impossible for us is not impossible for Him. He consistently uses seemingly "impossible" means in order to guarantee that the ends bring glory exclusively to Himself.

God has and does use Gentiles to bring Jewish people to faith, even in the post-Holocaust world. We may marvel over that fact, but we shouldn't deny that fact or doubt. And in light of that fact, we have to ask the final question:

4) Does the Holocaust, therefore, absolve Christians from testifying to Jewish people about the Lord today?

As I mentioned above, the all-too-frequent failure of the church to be a clear and loving witness to Israel has made it more difficult for Christians to gain an open hearing from the Jewish people. But increased difficulty doesn't remove God-given responsibility. Just because the church has corrupted her testimony in the past, she is not, therefore, free from the responsibility of testifying correctly in the present. In fact, I would say that *because* the church has failed so miserably in the past, she is under an even greater obligation to speak properly and more clearly at this present time.

God consistently uses seemingly "impossible" means in order to guarantee that the ends bring glory exclusively to Himself.

What a terrible thing it is if we use the sins of our past as a license and as an excuse to perform sins in the present. The Scriptures give an extremely grave admonition to believers who harbor a love for Israel and a burden for her well-being, but who refuse to express that love by declaring the message that God wants Israel to hear.

> "Now as for you, son of man, I have appointed you
> a watchman for the house of Israel; so you will hear

a message from My mouth and give them warning from Me. When I say to the wicked, 'O wicked man, you will surely die,' and you do not speak to warn the wicked from his way, that wicked man shall die in his iniquity, but his blood I will require from your hand." (Ezek. 33:7–8; see also 3:17–18)

These words were spoken to Ezekiel, but they apply to believers in this present age as well. In fact, these words speak to all believers about our responsibility to be witnesses not just to the Jewish people, but to everyone who needs to hear the good news.

Paul certainly understood that these words were a warning to believers in this present age. That's why he paraphrased them when he spoke to Jewish opponents in Corinth who not only resisted the message but blasphemed the name of the Lord. The Scriptures explain that "he shook out his garments and said to them, 'Your blood be on your own heads! I am clean'" (Acts 18:6). These words were not an imprecation or a curse but merely a solemn statement of a theological truth. It was not Paul's responsibility to convince the people to believe; it was his responsibility to present the claims clearly, lovingly, and consistently so that they may choose to receive or reject. Had he kept silent, their blood would have been on his head, just as the admonition in Ezekiel explains. But because he spoke, he was clean.

Clearly, Paul believed that the admonition in Ezekiel applied to himself, and he took the principle to heart. So should we.

CHAPTER 18

"Gentiles Can't Witness to Jews"

I've been told . . .

> "We non-Jewish Christians can't effectively share our faith with Jewish people, because we don't have the same credibility as Messianic Jews. And, we really don't have the responsibility. We're merely told to provoke the Jews to jealousy, and that's all."

THE THOUGHT THAT non-Jewish Christians can't effectively share their faith with us Jews simply isn't true. If you were to ask any handful of Jewish believers whether God used non-Jewish Christians in a significant way during their journeys of faith, the answer would be a resounding yes. So what's the source of this idea about "Gentile ineffectiveness"? It stems in part from a false notion of credibility.

"Surely a Jewish person can share the gospel more effectively with a fellow Jew, right?" Not necessarily. Very often, we Messianic Jews have no credible voice. We're written off as traitors. And no one likes traitors. In fact, it's not uncommon to find that the "higher" the position a Jewish person holds within the traditional Jewish community, the less credibility that person possesses if he or she comes to faith in Yeshua. Remember, God didn't use Saul of Tarsus, the student of Gamaliel, to be the apostle to us Jews. In fact, the Lord even forewarned Saul that the crowds in Jerusalem would not accept his testimony (Acts 22:18). Instead of using a brilliant rabbi named Saul, God used a common fisherman named Peter.

As for the rabbi Saul, better known as the apostle Paul, tradition tells us that he was frail and unattractive. Yet this is the person whom God sent to bring the gospel to a Gentile world that idolized beauty and strength.

Why would God choose a weak, unattractive intellectual to be the apostle to a world that worshiped power and physical form? And why would God choose a blue-collar fisherman to be the apostle to the Jewish religious elite?

Because that's what God does, so that He alone will get the glory. "God has chosen the foolish things of the world to shame the wise, and God has chosen the weak things of the world to shame the things which are strong" (1 Cor. 1:27).

A MARVELOUS PARTNERSHIP

The notion that Gentile Christians can't effectively share the gospel with Jews also stems from ignorance about the complementary roles that Messianic Jews and Gentile Christians play in bringing Jewish people to the Lord. It's a marvelous partnership and privilege.

So often, God will use a Jewish believer like me to arrest other Jewish people's attention. The dissonance of "Jews believing Jesus" captures their interest, sometimes as a curiosity, oftentimes as an initial offense. But either way, the interest is caught, and the Jewish person wants to know two things about Messianic Jews: what do we believe, and why do we believe it (perhaps even, how can we be so *foolish* as to believe it)? So this person will meet with us once, twice, or more, and we'll talk.

But what's missing from the person's list of questions? The most important question of all: "Is it *true*?" Once a Jewish person approaches that question, it's like stepping up to a threshold. And the person must either cross the threshold or step back. Crossing the threshold is risky, to say the least. It amounts to discovering that all this talk about Yeshua is true. Jesus really is the Messiah, and so we must believe no matter what it costs us in the end.

Often, the risk seems too daunting to face at first, and some Jewish people will invariably back away from the threshold. But they don't necessarily back away from the quest. They simply turn aside to the Gentile believer who poses no threat. The dialogue is seen as a cross-cultural exchange of views, nothing more. So the conversation continues in a climate where the Jewish seekers feel secure, while the Holy Spirit is convicting their hearts. Ultimately, the seekers know that it's true, and they know that a stand must be taken.

That's where one of us Messianic Jews often comes back into the picture. The Jewish inquirers are back at the threshold, staring through the opened door. They see us on the other side, they know they won't be alone if they cross the threshold, and that helps them take the step.

The notion that Gentile Christians can't effectively share their faith with Jewish people simply isn't true. But the notion that Gentile Christians are supposed to provoke us Jews to jealousy is absolutely true, and that's what the Bible explains: "Salvation has come to the Gentiles, to make them [Jews] jealous" (Rom. 11:11).

Provoking us Jews to jealousy is biblical, and it works! I know it works, because it worked in my own life. Before I surrendered my heart to Yeshua, God brought two types of believers into my life: "Jews for Jesus," and Gentile Christians. Both types of believers confronted me with the messianic claims of the Lord. But the non-Jewish Christians did something more; they made me jealous.

But jealous of what?

Jealous of their lifestyle? No, not really. I was happy with the lifestyle that I lived, and I had no reason to envy theirs.

Jealous of their culture? Not at all. I was born a Jew and I'll die a Jew. My Jewish culture has always been central to my very self-definition. I cherish my rich Jewish heritage.

So what made me jealous? Simply that they had a real relationship with a living God—the God of Israel, no less!

I was jealous of that relationship and of all the advantages that came with it. The reality of God's love. The certainty of His presence. The guarantee of His availability. The assurance of His forgiveness. The confidence of a purpose that was found in His will for their lives. And the gift of an eternal relationship with Him. I was jealous for what they had and what I lacked.

But how did I know about these things? Because they told me.

What if they hadn't? What if I'd come to them and said, "Tell me about this Jesus whom you think is the Jewish Messiah." And what if, in response, they'd said, "Oh, no. I'm not credible enough. I'm not effective. You need to talk to someone else."

Thankfully, they didn't put me off when I asked. And they didn't wait for me to ask. They looked for the opportunities to tell me what I needed to know. It was the telling as much as the seeing that awakened my interest, alerted me to my need, arrested my attention, and ultimately, provoked me to jealousy.

A HOLY TURNAROUND

Paul isn't the first biblical writer to talk about a ministry of provoking others to jealousy. Moses spoke of that ministry as well. Near the end of his life, he told God's people:

> "See, I have taught you statutes and judgments just as the LORD my God commanded me . . . So keep and do them, for that is your wisdom and your understanding in the sight of the peoples [Gentiles] who will hear all these statutes and say, 'Surely this great nation is a wise and understanding people.' For what great nation is there that has a god so near to it as is the LORD our God whenever we call on Him? Or what great nation is there that has statutes and judgments as righteous as this whole law which I am setting before you today?" (Deut. 4:5–8)

According to this passage, one of the reasons God gave us the Law of Moses was to make the surrounding nations envious of what we possessed: a God who is real, a God who is near, and a God who answers when we call. God gave us the Law to provoke the Gentiles to jealousy.

But they had to know what made them jealous. They had to hear of our statutes in order conclude, "Surely, this is a wise and understanding people." They had to know what we had and what they lacked.

The question isn't "who's more effective?" Rather, it's "what role does God want *me* to play in bringing His people back to Him?"

My people have the very same need today. If salvation has come to the nations in order to provoke us Jews to jealousy, then we need to know what you have and what we lack.

So, are Messianic Jews better witnesses to our fellow Jews than Christians from the nations? Are Christians from among the nations ineffective in sharing the gospel with us Jews? Does a non-Jewish Christian's responsibility consist of provoking us Jews to jealousy and nothing more?

Actually, these are the wrong questions to ask. The question isn't "who's more effective?" Rather, it's "what role does God want *me* to play in bringing His people back to Him?"

THE REAL REASONS
FOR CHOOSING
NOT TO SPEAK

CHAPTER 19

The Fear of Offending

I've been told . . .

> "If Christians endorse or take part in Jewish evangelism, Jewish leaders will take offense."

SADLY, THAT'S TRUE. But taking offense is not a particularly "Jewish" problem; it's a "human" problem. The gospel may always offend people who don't yet recognize the need to come to God on His terms and not their own. That some will be offended is unavoidable, but it's also biblical. And, in a heartening way, it's also evidence that the gospel is having its promised effect. For whenever the gospel is clearly proclaimed and understood, two results always occur: some people are convicted of their sins and drawn closer to God, while others are insulted and driven further away. That's why Paul told us that "we are a fragrance of Christ to God among those who are being saved and among those who are perishing; to the one an aroma from death to death, to the other an aroma from life to life" (2 Cor. 2:15–16).

THE UNAVOIDABLE OFFENSE

It's regrettable that endorsing or participating in Jewish evangelism will evoke the ire of some Jewish leaders. But it's a spiritual fact of life. Messianic Jews understand this, and we invariably have to wrestle with that fact early in our walk of faith. Though committed to maintaining our love for our people and our respect for those who lead them, we know that we must make a choice between heeding those Jewish leaders who oppose our faith, and heeding the Jewish Messiah who calls us to believe and follow. It's not a question of respecting those Jewish leaders less but of revering the Lord more.

The more diligently we seek to obtain God's favor through our own good deeds, the more vile and offensive is the message that declares, "Not good enough."

Undoubtedly, some non-Jewish Christians need to make a similar choice between acceding to Jewish leaders whom they admire and respect, and obeying the greatest Jewish leader of all, the Messiah Yeshua, who made it clear that the gospel must be preached to everyone, beginning with the house of Israel.

Jewish evangelism is offensive because the message of the gospel offends. That's why the apostle Paul, quoting the prophet Isaiah, wrote, "Behold, I lay in Zion a stone of stumbling and a rock of offense, and he who believes in Him will not be disappointed" (Rom. 9:33).

What's the offense? No matter how religiously we may live, and no matter how righteously we may act, we still fall woefully short of the glory of God. The more diligently we seek to obtain God's favor through our own good deeds, the more vile and offensive is the message that declares, "Not good enough."

Think for a moment about what might have fueled Saul's fury against the early church when, as a Hebrew of Hebrews, he followed the Law and our traditions more zealously than many of his contemporaries (Gal. 1:14). I suspect that much of that fury stemmed from the unspeakably offensive gospel claim that he would never know God's pardon or favor until he repented and trusted not in his own meticulous observance, but in the righteousness of an uneducated carpenter from the backwater slums of Galilee. How offensive the gospel must have seemed to Saul of Tarsus!

The gospel is offensive, and this is why we must proclaim the gospel in love. But no matter how lovingly we endeavor to present the good news, the naked reality of the bad news—that we're sinners who have offended God—will always bring about either the pain of righteous conviction or the pain of self-righteous indignation.

The key does not lie in seeking to eliminate the offense of the cross. The key lies in making certain that if offense is taken, it is taken because of the clarity of the message and not because of the callousness of the messenger. The apostle Peter had some good words for us on that particular point: "Make sure that none of you suffers as a murderer, or thief, or evildoer, or troublesome meddler; but if anyone suffers as a Christian, he is not to be ashamed" (1 Peter 4:15–16).

Have you ever noticed that there were

The bad news—that we're sinners who have offended God—will always bring about either the pain of righteous conviction or the pain of self-righteous indignation.

times when Jesus spoke so indelicately that the leaders of the Jewish people couldn't help but take offense at what He said? In Matthew 15:1–9, we read that certain scribes and Pharisees challenged Yeshua with the question, "Why do Your disciples break the traditions of the elders?" Yeshua countered their challenge with a very stern rebuke: "Why do you yourselves transgress the commandment of God for the sake of your tradition?" The disciples' words to Jesus tell us precisely how these Pharisees felt about what Jesus said. "Do You know that the Pharisees were offended when they heard this statement?" (Matt. 15:12).

But I can also think of times recorded in the Gospels when He performed miracles that demonstrated nothing but the vastness of His unconditional love, like the raising of Lazarus from the dead. Who could take offense? And yet, the Scripture makes it clear that even in that instance, certain religious leaders were offended to the point of making plans to bring about His death (John 11:45–48, 53).

Why were they offended? I suspect it was for two reasons. First, these leaders realized that they were losing the battle for the hearts of the common people, and so they were jealous (v. 48). And second, these leaders understood what the miracles meant: yes, Jesus is love, but Jesus is also Lord.

Love is no guarantee that someone will not take offense to the gospel message, the lordship of Yeshua, or the cross. So let's learn to be wary of causing ungodly offense. But let's not live in fear of the offense that's inherent in the gospel message. Let's not dread the offense that's always taken by someone when that message finds its voice.

Perhaps you'll be encouraged if I tell you that so many Jewish believers in Jesus—myself included—were deeply, painfully offended when we first heard and understood what the gospel message said. But God turned the offense of the cross into conviction from the Holy Spirit.

And by the grace of God, we believed!

CHAPTER 20

The Fear of Rejection, the Fear of Man

AN HONEST EXAMINATION of the Scriptures must lead us to the conclusion—whether comfortable or not—that we Jews need Jesus and His gospel in order to be saved. Why then is it so hard for some Christians to endorse that truth in an open way? What's the struggle and the fear? The real question that so many people find distressing is not, "Do Jews need to believe in Jesus in order to be saved?" but rather, "How can I endorse this difficult truth without facing the threat of being scorned, despised, and rejected by my Jewish friends?" The simple answer is that you can't avoid the risk. And the risk of rejection will undoubtedly become the reality in some cases, though not in all.

But just as we Jews who've believed in Yeshua needed to make some difficult choices, so our non-Jewish brothers and sisters in the faith need to make some difficult choices as well—to choose not just to believe but to identify with Him, despite the rejection that the identification always brings. Scripture tells us that "He was despised and forsaken of men"

(Isa. 53:3). Jesus informs us that this rejection will be ours as well, for "If they persecuted Me, they will also persecute you" (John 15:20). Jesus commands us to take up our cross and embrace the reality of that rejection if we truly intend to follow Him (Luke 9:23). Jesus warns us of the consequences of putting our fear of rejection above our open and unashamed fidelity to the Lord. "For whoever is ashamed of Me and My words, the Son of Man will be ashamed of him when He comes in His glory" (Luke 9:26).

Gentile believers who love the Jewish people need to choose *how* to love us. They can love us with a "human" love that desires to be loved back more than anything else. That kind of love makes reciprocal love the greatest goal. As a result, that kind of love can compromise the truth, if the truth may cause rejection. Or believers in Jesus can love their Jewish friends with a godly love that cares more for the welfare of the beloved than about the possible outcome of openly endorsing an unpopular truth. A godly love places the well-being of the beloved above the likely consequences of speaking the truth in love. This is how Moses and the prophets loved us. This is how the apostles loved us. This is how Jesus loved my people when He walked among us on earth, and this is how He loves us today. He loves us enough to bring the gospel into our lives, despite the rejection that it so often brings about.

> Believers in Jesus can love their Jewish friends with a godly love that cares more for the welfare of the beloved than about the possible outcome of openly endorsing an unpopular truth.

If you are a non-Jewish Christian, I hope you'll choose to love the Jewish people with a godly love. I hope you'll choose to love my people enough to pray for their salvation and to advocate with an open voice my people's need to receive the Savior's forgiveness and gift of eternal life.

I can't promise that you won't face scorn and rejection from some Jewish people as well as from some people in the church. But many will respect your honesty, even though they disagree. Many will love you and thank God for you, after they come to faith.

I can promise more. I can promise that you won't endure the rejection alone. Jesus will stand right beside you, because any rejection you may face is ultimately directed at Him (Luke 10:16). And He can turn any person who initially rejects the gospel into a person who not only accepts the good news, but who advocates for it. Look at what He did with the apostle Paul.

We Jews who believe in Jesus will stand beside you as well. We'll stand beside you and love you for doing the right thing. We'll stand beside you with admiration for choosing the correct and courageous route. We'll stand beside you with an unending gratitude to the Lord for the part you'll play in returning the lost sheep of the house of Israel to the Shepherd of our souls.

Postscript

A Personal Invitation

IF YOU'RE NOT YET a believer in Yeshua, then I'd like to thank you for reading what I've written, and I'd like to leave you with an earnest and openhearted request. Would you be willing to find out if the gospel message is actually true? The claims of Scripture can be hard to hear. The Bible even tells us that "As a result of this [the difficulty of accepting Jesus' words] many of His disciples withdrew and were not walking with Him anymore" (John 6:66). But would you be willing to look at the matter with an open mind? And if you discover that it's true, would you be willing to believe in Him and follow Him openly, despite the consequences that you'll probably bring on yourself? We Jews who've made that discovery and who've made that choice know that it's not easy. But every one of us needs to decide what matters more: the approval of people, or the approval of God.

If you've never believed and you have some questions, I'd like to invite you to contact me so that we can carry on the discussion that you and I have already started by virtue of your reading what I've written so far. You can email me at avi.snyder@jewsforjesus.org. I'll be happy to be in touch.

However, if you already know that the gospel is true, but

you've never taken a moment to repent and ask the Lord to forgive you, I'd like to invite you to do that right now, just by echoing in your heart the words of this prayer:

Lord Yeshua, I know that I've sinned. I know that my life doesn't please You. I know that I deserve Your wrath. But I believe that You love me. I believe that You died as the payment for my sins and then rose from the dead so that I might have an intimate, everlasting relationship with You. Please forgive me. Please rescue me. Please make me one of Your own, and I will follow You. Amen.

If you've said and believe that prayer, would you let me know so that I can connect you with other believers in your area?

Acknowledgments

OF THE MANY PEOPLE who encouraged me, I'd especially like to thank Irmhild Bärend, who told me that this book would not be written unless I made the time to write it. I'd also like to express my special thanks to my friends and colleagues Susan Perlman, Rich Robinson, Ruth Rosen, and Matt Sieger, for their input, care, and advice.

Finding *Christ* IN THE *Old Testament*

Find the connection between the ancient fall festival of the Old Testament and Jesus Christ.

978-0-8024-1402-1

Behold the excitement leading up to the Feast of Pentacost and the richness it will bring to your understanding of both the Old and New Testament.

978-0-8024-1402-1

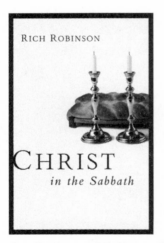

Explore the themes of Shabbat in all of Scripture, and then discover what it has meant to Jews and Christians for centuries.

978-0-8024-1199-0

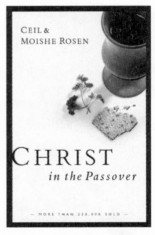

Learn how the death and resurrection of Jesus the Messiah are forever interwoven with the Passover and its symbolism.

978-0-8024-1389-5

IF YOU'RE CONVINCED THAT JEWS **DO** NEED JESUS...

...then here are some ways you can effectively share your faith with Jewish people:

- Get answers to your questions online by going to: **jewsforjesus.org/livechat** or write to us (see address below).

- Offer your Jewish friend an introductory subscription to *ISSUES*, our bi-monthly publication for Jewish seekers. (See sample online here http://j4j.co/offerissues.) We will not include your name in the offer unless you would like us to.

- Get your own copy of *Witnessing To Jews* by Jews for Jesus founder Moishe Rosen, which comes with a companion DVD, great role-playing examples, and a study guide—all for just $8 (retail value $15).

- Sign up for our free newsletter for Christians, where we provide regular teaching help, motivational stories of how Jewish people hear and respond to the gospel, and more.

Jews for Jesus
60 Haight Street, San Francisco, CA 94102

witnessing@jewsforjesus.org

JEWS FØR JESUS

established 32 A.D., give or take a year

WHAT OTHERS ARE SAYING:

"If I had two lives to live, I would spend the first one fulfilling my present calling. Then in my second life I would apply for a position with Jews for Jesus."

RAY ORTLUND JR., SENIOR PASTOR, IMMANUEL CHURCH, NASHVILLE

"I'm so glad to give my hearty endorsement to the work of Jews for Jesus."

JONI EARECKSON TADA, FOUNDER, CEO, JONI AND FRIENDS INTERNATIONAL

"I love their direct, unapologetic, one-to-one approach to evangelism. No one better understands how to present our Messiah to Jewish people."

JAY SEKULOW, CHIEF COUNSEL, AMERICAN CENTER FOR LAW AND JUSTICE

Evangelism is at the heart of Jews for Jesus. With a staff of 200, located in 26 cities in 14 countries, Jews for Jesus has conducted over 300 evangelistic campaigns, distributed more than 23 million pieces of evangelistic literature, and had one-on-one visits with over 100,00 Jewish people. In the past year alone they had 20,000 conversations online through live chat—all to make sure that Jews around the world know it is possible for a Jewish person to believe in Jesus as the promised Messiah of Israel and Savior of the world.

Avi Snyder invites you to join the Jews for Jesus adventure today!

CHECK OUT JEWSFORJESUS. ORG/JDNJ
